Your own Web site
on the Internet

BOOKS AVAILABLE

By both authors:

BP327 DOS one step at a time
BP337 A Concise User's Guide to Lotus 1-2-3 for Windows
BP341 MS-DOS explained
BP346 Programming in Visual Basic for Windows
BP352 Excel 5 explained
BP362 Access one step at a time
BP387 Windows one step at a time
BP388 Why not personalise your PC
BP400 Windows 95 explained
BP406 MS Word 95 explained
BP407 Excel 95 explained
BP408 Access 95 one step at a time
BP409 MS Office 95 one step at a time
BP415 Using Netscape on the Internet*
BP420 E-mail on the Internet*
BP426 MS-Office 97 explained
BP428 MS-Word 97 explained
BP429 MS-Excel 97 explained
BP430 MS-Access 97 one step at a time
BP433 Your own Web site on the Internet
BP448 Lotus SmartSuite 97 explained
BP456 Windows 98 explained*
BP460 Using Microsoft Explorer 4 on the Internet*
BP464 E-mail and news with Outlook Express
BP465 Lotus SmartSuite Millennium explained
BP471 Microsoft Office 2000 explained
BP472 Microsoft Word 2000 explained
BP473 Microsoft Excel 2000 explained
BP474 Microsoft Access 2000 explained
BP478 Microsoft Works 2000 explained

By Noel Kantaris:

BP258 Learning to Program in C
BP259 A Concise Introduction to UNIX*
BP284 Programming in QuickBASIC
BP325 A Concise User's Guide to Windows 3.1

Your own Web site on the Internet

by

P.R.M. Oliver
and
N. Kantaris

BERNARD BABANI (publishing) LTD.
THE GRAMPIANS
SHEPHERDS BUSH ROAD
LONDON W6 7NF
ENGLAND

PLEASE NOTE

Although every care has been taken with the production of this book to ensure that any projects, designs, modifications and/or programs, etc., contained herewith, operate in a correct and safe manner and also that any components specified are normally available in Great Britain, the Publishers and Author(s) do not accept responsibility in any way for the failure (including fault in design) of any project, design, modification or program to work correctly or to cause damage to any equipment that it may be connected to or used in conjunction with, or in respect of any other damage or injury that may be so caused, nor do the Publishers accept responsibility in any way for the failure to obtain specified components.

Notice is also given that if equipment that is still under warranty is modified in any way or used or connected with home-built equipment then that warranty may be void.

© 1998 BERNARD BABANI (publishing) LTD

First Published - December 1998
Reprinted - May 1999
Reprinted - October 1999
Reprinted - March 2000
Reprinted - October 2000

British Library Cataloguing in Publication Data:

A catalogue record for this book is available from the
British Library

ISBN 0 85934 433 9

Cover Design by Gregor Arthur
Cover illustration by Adam Willis
Printed and Bound in Great Britain by Cox & Wyman Ltd, Reading

ABOUT THIS BOOK

These days you can't read a paper, watch television, or even walk along the street, for very long before you see details of a company advertising their Web site on the Internet. It certainly has become an integral part of our lives over the last few years. If you want to join the bandwagon and quickly get up and running with your own Internet Web site to get your 'message' over to the rest of the world, this book *Your own Web site on the Internet* is definitely for you.

We step through the procedure of building an actual site. No previous knowledge of the Internet is assumed, so that anyone should be able to follow the book without too much trouble, but we do not cover in any detail how to 'surf the net', how to set up your computer hardware, or how to install and use Windows. If you need to know more about these, then may we suggest you select an appropriate book from the 'Books Available' list at the front. They are all published by BERNARD BABANI (publishing) Ltd.

An attempt has been made in the book not to use too much computer 'jargon', but with this subject, some is inevitable, so a large glossary of terms is included, which can be used with the text where necessary, or just as a reference.

To set the scene, the book starts with a very short history of the Internet and the World Wide Web and the potential benefits of advertising your presence to the world.

The next chapter dives in at the deep end with an explanation of what you will need to get up and running on the Internet. This includes what hardware you will need, how to get your Internet Service Provider, choosing a 'Domain' name, and the type of software that is available, for very little cost. Chapters follow on whether to get a professional to design and build your Web pages, or whether to take the much cheaper option of doing it yourself.

We then work through the steps of building a simple example Web site and publishing it on the Internet. This is done first using a fully WYSIWYG editor, and then after an introduction to HTML itself, using an HTML editor. If you want you can even build this site yourself.

Once your site is up and running how do you promote it so that people will come and take a look? If you get this wrong you will really have been wasting your time. With this in mind, the importance of search engines and how to get your site to appear at the top end of their result listings is covered in some detail. Then follows a section on keeping your site alive, and maintaining your Web pages on the server.

One thing to remember when reading the book is that the whole Internet scenario is changing every day, especially the Web. What is there to look at today, may have gone, or changed shape, by tomorrow. Hopefully the sites we point to in our text will still be there for you, but there are no guarantees.

Like the rest of our computer series, this book was written with the busy person in mind. It is not necessary to learn all there is to know about a subject, when reading a few concise pages can usually do the same thing quite adequately. With the help of this book, it is hoped that you will be able to come to terms with running your own site on the Internet and get the most out of your computer, and that you will be able to do it in the shortest, most effective and informative way. Good luck, and most important, enjoy yourself.

If you would like to purchase a Companion Disc for any of the listed books by the same authors, **apart from the ones marked with an asterisk**, containing the file/program listings which appear in them, then fill in the form at the back of the book and send it to Phil Oliver at the address given.

ABOUT THE AUTHORS

Noel Kantaris graduated in Electrical Engineering at Bristol University and after spending three years in the Electronics Industry in London, took up a Tutorship in Physics at the University of Queensland. Research interests in Ionospheric Physics, led to the degrees of M.E. in Electronics and Ph.D. in Physics. On return to the UK, he took up a Post-Doctoral Research Fellowship in Radio Physics at the University of Leicester, and then in 1973 a lecturing position in Engineering at the Camborne School of Mines, Cornwall, (part of Exeter University), where between 1978 and 1997 he was also the CSM Computing Manager. At present he is IT Director of FFC Ltd.

Phil Oliver graduated in Mining Engineering at Camborne School of Mines in 1967 and since then has specialised in most aspects of surface mining technology, with a particular emphasis on computer related techniques. He has worked in Guyana, Canada, several Middle Eastern countries, South Africa and the United Kingdom, on such diverse projects as: the planning and management of bauxite, iron, gold and coal mines; rock excavation contracting in the UK; international mining equipment sales and international mine consulting for a major mining house in South Africa. In 1988 he took up a lecturing position at Camborne School of Mines (part of Exeter University) in Surface Mining and Management. He retired from full-time lecturing in 1998, to spend more time writing, consulting and developing Web sites for clients.

ACKNOWLEDGEMENTS

We would like to thank friends and colleagues for the helpful tips and suggestions which assisted us in the writing of this book.

We would also like to thank the many Web site authors that have placed specialist information on their pages for us all to benefit from, especially:

Danny Sullivan for the comprehensive site, Search Engine Watch, located at

http://searchenginewatch.com/

Jim Wilson at Virtual Promote, who provides 'First aid for the walking wounded of Web site promotion'

http://www.virtualpromote.com/

x

TRADEMARKS

HP and LaserJet are registered trademarks of Hewlett Packard Corporation.

IBM is a registered trademark of International Business Machines, Inc.

Intel is a registered trademark of Intel Corporation.

Microsoft, **MS-DOS**, **Windows**, **Windows NT**, **Works**, and **Visual Basic**, are either registered trademarks or trademarks of Microsoft Corporation.

All other brand and product names used in the book are recognised as trademarks, or registered trademarks, of their respective companies.

CONTENTS

1. THE INTERNET

What is the Internet?

If you are reading this book you are obviously interested in how the Internet can be of help to you. Be assured that whatever your interests are, it certainly can be productively used, once you know a little about how to go about it. But first to set the scene, a few pages on how it all started

The Internet is an enormous international network linking computers of all shapes and sizes around the globe, allowing them to share and exchange resources, such as files and data. It has grown to its present form over the last thirty years, and some idea of its history may help to understand the nature of the beast.

A Brief History:

In the mid 1960s with the cold war very prominent in the Northern Hemisphere, the US military faced a strange strategic problem. How could the country successfully communicate after a possible nuclear attack? They would need a command and control communication network linking the cities, states and military bases, etc. But, no matter how the network was protected it would always be vulnerable to the impact of a nuclear attack and if the network had a control centre it would be the first to go.

As a solution, the concept was developed that the network itself should be assumed to be unreliable at all times and should be designed to overcome this unreliability. To achieve this, all the nodes of the network would be equal in status, each with its own authority to originate, pass, and receive messages. The messages themselves would be divided into small parts, or packets, with each being separately addressed. The transmission of each packet of data would begin at a specified source node, and end at another specified destination node, but would find its own way through the network, with the route taken being unimportant. With this concept, if sections of the network were destroyed, that wouldn't matter as the packets would use the surviving parts.

The National Physical Laboratory, here in the UK, set up the first test network on these principles in 1968. Shortly afterwards, the Pentagon's Advanced Research Projects Agency (ARPA) funded a larger, more ambitious project in the USA, with the high-speed 'supercomputers' of the day as the network nodes.

In 1969, the first such node was installed in UCLA. By December of that year, there were four nodes on the infant network, which was named ARPANET, after its sponsor. The four computers could transfer data on dedicated high-speed transmission lines, and could be programmed remotely from the other nodes. For the first time, scientists and researchers could share one another's computer facilities from a long distance. By 1972 there were thirty-seven nodes in ARPANET.

It soon became apparent, however, that much of the traffic on ARPANET was not long-distance computing, but consisted of news and personal messages. Researchers were using ARPANET not only to collaborate on projects and trade ideas on work, but to socialise. They had their own personal accounts on the ARPANET computers, and their own personal addresses for electronic mail and they were very enthusiastic about this particular new service, e-mail.

Throughout the '70s, the ARPA network grew. Its decentralised structure made expansion easy as it could accommodate different types of computers, as long as they could speak the standard packet-switching language. ARPA's original standard for communication was known as NCP short for 'Network Control Protocol', but this was soon superseded by the higher-level standard known as TCP/IP, which has survived until today.

TCP, or 'Transmission Control Protocol', converts messages into streams of packets at the source, then re-assembles them back into messages at the destination. IP, or 'Internet Protocol', handles the addressing.

Over the years, ARPANET itself became a smaller and smaller part of the growing proliferation of other networked machines, but TCP/IP continued to link them all. As the '70s and '80s advanced, many different groups found themselves in possession of powerful computers and that it was fairly easy to link these computers to the growing global network. As the use of TCP/IP, which was in the public-domain by that time, became more common, entire other networks were incorporated into the **Internet**.

In 1984 the National Science Foundation became involved and created the new NSFNET linking newer and faster supercomputers with bigger and faster links. Other US government agencies joined the bandwagon, including NASA, the National Institutes of Health and the Department of Energy.

ARPANET itself formally died in 1989, but its functions not only continued but were steadily improved. In Europe, major international 'backbone' networks started to provide connectivity to many millions of computers on a large number of other networks. Commercial network providers in both the US, Europe and Asia were beginning to offer Internet access and support on a competitive basis to any interested parties.

The extended use of the Internet cost the original founders little or nothing extra, since each new node was independent, and had to handle its own technical requirements and funding.

The Internet Today:

Today there are hundreds of thousands of nodes in the Internet, scattered throughout the world, with more coming on-line all the time and many millions of people using this often named 'Information Super Highway' every day.

Built to be 'indestructible' and with no centralised control, it's no wonder the word 'anarchic' is often bandied around by the media when the Internet is discussed!

Right, enough of the history lesson, we will now work through the stages of designing and setting up your own site on the Internet, and hopefully give you a few pointers on getting people to visit it.

We will do this by going through the stages of developing an actual small three page Web site. You can follow the stages yourself, if you like, by duplicating the site. Or you can simply read about it, the choice is yours.

2. USING THE INTERNET

Why Use the Internet?

Now we know what the Internet is, what can we use it for? For most people there are two uses:

- sending and receiving e-mail messages
- using the World Wide Web (or Web for short) to access and transfer data stored on other computers, which can be located anywhere in the World. This book will concentrate on this aspect of the Internet and will step you through the process of setting up your own Web site.

E-mail:

Electronic mail has to be the main use of the Internet. It is very much faster that letter mail, which is known as 'snailmail' by regular e-mail users. It consists of electronic text, that is transmitted, sometimes in seconds, to anywhere else in the World that is connected to a main network. E-mail can also be used to send software and data files by attaching the files to a message.

File Transfers:

There is a fantastic amount of free software available over the Internet, as well as a multitude of text and graphic files on most subjects you care to mention.

File transfers can be carried out with a protocol known as FTP, which allows Internet users to access remote machines and retrieve them for their own use. Many Internet computers allow anyone to access them anonymously, and to simply copy their public files, free of charge. With the right connections, entire books can be transferred in a matter of minutes. With the wrong connections though, the process can take hours! Of course, many more millions of files are available to people with accounts, who are prepared to pay for them.

We will discuss using FTP later in the book, as this is the main way to transfer your Web pages from your own PC to your Web site located on a distant server.

Up until recently all of these activities required very expensive computing facilities and a large measure of computer literacy. Times have changed, however, and it is now possible to fairly easily and cheaply install a modem in your PC, connect to the Internet and with a Web browser, like Netscape Navigator, or Microsoft Explorer, carry them out with very little technical knowledge. If you buy a new PC now it will almost certainly come fully equipped with all you will need for this.

The World Wide Web

The World Wide Web, WWW, W3, or Web as we shall call it, has been responsible for the rapidly expanding popularity of the Internet. When you see the Internet being accessed on TV, what you actually see is a Web page being read on a PC. A Web site is made up of a group of Web pages, all stored on an Internet server. The Web consisting of many millions of such sites, located on server computers around the globe, all of which you can access with the browser software on your own PC. Hopefully, with the help of this book you should easily be able to set up your own Web site for the rest of the world to access. But first a little more background information, which of course you can skip if you really want to.

The Web was initially developed in Switzerland by CERN (the European Laboratory for Particle Physics), to form a distributed hypermedia system. It now consists of Web client computers (yours and mine) and server computers handling multimedia documents with hypertext links built into them (Web pages). Client

6

computers use browser software (such as Navigator and Explorer) to view pages of these documents, one at a time. Server computers use Web server software to maintain the documents for us to access.

If you have used the Help pages of Microsoft Windows you are familiar with a hypertext document. It contains links that you click with the mouse pointer to jump to other information. The advantage of hypertext in a Web document is that if you want more information about a particular subject, you just click on a hypertext link and another page is opened for you to read, view or listen to. Documents can be linked to other documents (or graphics, movies or sound files) by completely different authors and stored in completely different computers; much like footnoting, but you can get the referenced document instantly!

So, to access the Web, you run a browser program which reads files and documents, and fetches them from other sources on the Internet into the memory of your PC. Thus Web browsers provide users a consistent means of accessing a variety of media in a very simplified fashion. They have changed the way people view and create information, and have formed the first true global hypermedia network. No wonder their use has taken off so dramatically in the last few years.

Hypermedia is a superset of hypertext - it is any medium with pointers to other media. This means that the latest browsers display formatted text, images, play sound clips, or even video type animations. Some of these, however, may require extra hardware, like a sound card, on your computer.

To create your own Web pages and build a site is a fairly easy process, as we shall see, but there are two areas you will need to work on if you want to really master the subject. These are the HTML language and an understanding of URL link addresses.

HTML - The Web Language:

Web pages are actually text documents created by authors using a language called 'HyperText Markup Language', or HTML for short. This offers short codes, or tags, to control text, designate graphical elements and hypertext links. Clicking a link on a Web page in your browser, brings documents located on a distant server to your screen, irrespective of the server's geographic location. Documents may contain text, images, sounds, movies, or a combination of these, in other words - multimedia. All of these are 'built into' a Web page with HTML code.

There are many software packages around to help you build Web pages, and you can go a long way using some of these without knowing HTML. To get your pages to look the way you want, however, you will need some knowledge, as discussed in a later chapter.

URLs and how Links are Named:

Every link in a hypertext Web document has to have a unique name and you will need to understand about Uniform Resource Locators, or URLs. It is possible to represent any file or service on the Internet with a URL address and we give several examples below.

The first part of the URL (before the two slashes) specifies the method of access. The second is the domain address of the Web site. Further parts may specify the names of files, the port to connect to, or the text to search for in a database. A URL is always a single unbroken line **with no spaces**.

8

Here are some examples of URLs:

http://www.ex.ac.uk/location/book.html

This would connect to an HTTP server (a Web server) and would retrieve an HTML file (a Web file) called *book.html* from a directory called *location* found on the Web server at the University of Exeter, in the UK.

ftp://xerox.com/pub/file.txt

This would open an FTP connection to the domain name xerox.com and retrieve a text file.

http://www.michaelstrang.com/

This, as we shall see, is a real address and will open onto the home page of the Web site we are using as an example for the rest of the book.

The first part of the URL (before the two slashes) gives the method of access at that address:

- **http** - a hypertext document or directory
- **gopher** - a Gopher document or menu
- **ftp** - (file transfer protocol) a file available for downloading or a directory of such files
- **news** - a newsgroup
- **Telnet** - a computer system that you can log into from across the Internet
- **WAIS** - a database or document on a WAIS (**W**ide **A**rea **I**nformation **S**earch) database
- **file** - a file located on a local drive (like the C: hard drive, or disc, on your own PC)

Sites that run Web servers are typically named with a www at the beginning of the network address.

When you click on a hypertext link in a Web page (an HTML document), you are actually sending a request to open that URL and have the named data file copied to your PC. In this way, hyperlinks can be made not only to other texts and media, but also to other network services. Web browsers are not simply Web clients, but are also full FTP, Gopher, and Telnet clients in their own rights.

All of these features are now readily available over ordinary phone lines, once you get Internet access through a local Internet Service Provider, as explained in the next chapter.

3. GETTING ON LINE

As we shall see in the next chapter, there are several ways you can go about getting your own Web site. You can have it all done for you, or get more involved and spend a few more days doing it yourself. In either case there are some basic requirements you will need. For both you will need a computer which is connected to the Internet, but before you can do anything about building your own site you will also need suitable software to help build and service your Web pages.

Hardware Requirements

If you have recently bought a new PC you should have no problems regarding its power. Entry models now are extremely powerful and getting remarkably 'cheap'.

For an older model, the minimum hardware requirements to run Windows and a browser, etc., are a 486, or higher, PC with 8 MB of RAM, a SVGA Display with at least 256 colours or preferably higher, and at least 6 to 10 MB of spare hard disc space. You will also need a connection to the Internet, via a Modem, Ethernet Card, or ISDN direct phone line.

To run a version of Netscape, or Microsoft Explorer as an on-line browser you must have a suitable Internet connection. The ability to send and receive e-mail does not necessarily mean you will be able to access the World Wide Web. There are three requirements for this:

1   A direct Ethernet connection to the net, or a dialup SLIP or PPP account from an Internet service provider (ISP).

2   A TCP/IP stack.

3   The browser software.

Getting your Web Connection

Unless you are lucky enough to have a PC which is connected to a Local Area Network (LAN) which has Internet access, you will need a modem to be able to communicate with the rest of the world. This is a device that converts data so that it can be transmitted over the telephone system.

You will also need to find, and subscribe to, a suitable Internet provider. There are many such providers in the UK. Most can be listed on the Web by accessing the following address:

http://thelist.internet.com/

and looking under the UK, or wherever else you are based. Another way would be to buy an Internet based PC magazine from your local newsagent and look at the reviews and adverts. Also you could try your telephone directory, or possibly adverts in the computer section of your local paper. Be careful though before committing yourself to one provider as the quality of service and costs can vary considerably. One thing we can't do here is make specific recommendations, but try and find someone who uses the company you decide on, or have a trial period with them.

What you are ideally looking for is **full dial-up SLIP or PPP connection with unlimited WWW access to the Internet**, and this should be possible by dialling a local number to your provider's access point. (SLIP and PPP are only two communication standards that you need to have, but do not need to understand).

The local call access will mean your phone bills should not be excessive, especially if you do your Web accessing in off-peak times. The unlimited access means you will not pay any extra to your Internet Provider no matter how many hours you spend on line, just your monthly fee.

At least 5MB, but preferably 10MB, of Web server space should also be provided for you. This is where you will install you Web site, once you have designed and built it. A few other services that will be required here are:

- Unlimited data transfer, uploads and downloads. Some providers charge extra if your site gets too popular and uses too much 'bandwidth'.

- The possibility of having your own Domain Name but this will cost extra to register.

- Free access via FTP for 24 hours per day, so that you can set up your site pages and make changes to them whenever you want to.

- At least 1 POP e-mail account and the possibility of setting up e-mail forwarding accounts and aliases.

- Some other goodies that you may find useful are, hit counters, Server Side Includes (SSI) support, your own cgi-bin directory and access to CGI, JavaScript and image libraries.

If these things don't mean much to you at the moment please do not panic, if necessary we will explain them as we go along. A service, like that described above, will probably cost in the region of £10 per month, and there may well be a setting up charge as well.

If you need to purchase and install a modem, your Internet Provider should be able to recommend or even provide one, along with all the necessary cables, connections, software, help and back up that is bound to be required.

From now on in this book, we assume that you have an active connection to your Service Provider and the Internet. Trouble shooting this cannot be within our remit!

Domain Names

In the last chapter we showed how Web pages and files all had their own URL address on the Internet. We saw that part of this address consisted of the domain name of the site owner. So domain names are the names used to conveniently contact an Internet site or e-mail address. Without domain names contacting an Internet site would require you to know the IP address (Internet Protocol) of the site, such as:

209.63.61.131

Until recently, this IP address was that of one of our sites with the domain name:

michaelstrang.com

Which of these has more meaning to you and which would be the easiest to remember? Computers, on the other hand, are quite happy with more complex numbers. Whenever you click a link on a Web page, a request is sent to a server on the international system known as the Domain Name Service (DNS), which translates the easier to remember domain name in the URL to the less friendly IP address that is required to connect to the linked site.

Your Own Domain Name:

Your Internet Service Provider should give you a domain name (of sorts) when you sign up. By default this will include his name, as well as your personal identifier, such as www.yourname.providername.co.uk. If this doesn't bother you, no problem.

There are, however, some advantages to having your very own virtual domain name like ours above, but you will, of course, have to pay extra for them.

- The name can be much shorter, easier to remember and relevant to your needs.
- It is completely personalised.

- Once it is registered and as long as you pay the fees, you will have unique use of that name no matter what server your Web site is on, or where it is located.

If, for example, your UK based company was called XYZ123 Ltd you may be able to register any of the following domain names:

xyz123.co.uk
xyz123.ltd.uk
xyz123.com
xyz123.net

You should first check to see if the name you want to use is still available, maybe from the site shown below:

http://www.1stnames.co.uk/

Domain Name Registration Rules:

The only characters that are allowed in the main body of a domain name are letters, digits and a hyphen (-), but it cannot end in a hyphen.

A Domain name may not contain any spaces, and must be between 3 and 26 characters long.

Any person or company may own any number of domain names with the **.co.uk** or **.com** suffixes as long as they continue to pay to keep the registration.

.ltd.uk, and **.plc.uk** names are for use by companies registered with Companies House, each company may only register the name that corresponds to their registered company name, excluding the Limited or plc part of their company name.

.net.uk, and **.net** names are intended only for use by organisations involved in the provision of Internet services.

.org.uk, and **.org** names are intended for use by non-profit making organisations. Only one should be registered for the same organisation.

Registering your Domain Name:

Once you have decided on a name and checked that it is free, you have to register it. You could let your Web space provider do this for you, or else use one of the many 'registration' Web sites available. A search for 'domain names' will lead you to these. The one shown on the previous page may well come up.

You will of course have to pay. Registering sites in the UK seems to be more expensive than doing it in the USA. Here it may cost well in excess of £100 for the first two years use of your name. In the US, at the moment, it is about $70, having recently been reduced. Our *michaelstrang.com* site was registered, and is actually located, on a server in the States. We found it much cheaper and easier to do it that way.

Some Useful Software

At this stage you do not have to go overboard with buying a lot of software programs, but there are some that you will need. All of those described here can be downloaded from the Internet and used straight away.

Some programs are **shareware** and will require a payment in the future after you have tried them out. This will keep you legal and goes towards paying for the program development. Others may be **Freeware** and have been released by their authors so that anyone can use them free of charge.

Pre-release, or **beta**, software is also free to everyone. By using a beta test version, you have an opportunity to work with the next generation of software before it is officially released. But be warned, it may only operate for a limited period.

Web Browsers:

Before you can access the Web you will need a browser. These days that means a version of either Microsoft Explorer or one from Netscape. Most Internet Service Providers should provide you with one of these as part of their package. If not, you can easily obtain the latest versions on-line from either of the companies. Explorer seems to come bundled with all of Microsoft's large software packages these days, and is actually part of Windows 98. Be warned though, this program seems to take over your computer. We much prefer Netscape browsers and very much hope that Bill Gates does not succeed in putting them out of business!

The Netscape browsers we use are Communicator ver 4.04 and Navigator Gold version 3.04. These both have a WYSIWYG editor built in so that you can build Web pages visually, without having to know any HTML code. With them you can also save other people's Web pages to your hard disc, complete with all the graphics.

This can be very useful if you want to know how they programmed their page, or want to 'borrow' some of their features! Version 3.04 is not a current version but, at the time of writing, was still available to download from:

ftp://archive.netscape.com/archive/index.html

You can download the Communicator from Netscape by accessing their home page at:

http://www.netscape.com

and following the **Netscape Download** link. Another source is the CD-ROMs you can buy with some of today's computer magazines.

HTML Editors:

HTML, or HyperText Markup Language, as we saw in a previous chapter, is the language used for writing pages for the Web. HTML Editors assist the author by providing menu options, buttons and icons that insert the necessary HTML tags. The page being built is still shown in ASCII, or text, format, so you need to know the basics of HTML, but the actual markup code is placed for you. Some of them are like an upmarket version of Notepad. Once you understand a little HTML, one of these editors is ideal for writing your Web pages, or for 'tweaking' a page you have drafted in a WYSIWYG editor, like Netscape Composer.

There are many of these programs available to download. A favourite site of ours for finding extra Internet software is run by TUCOWS Interactive Limited, and it is well worth taking a look at one of their sites. If you are thinking of downloading anything from the Internet you should try and find the nearest site to you that you can so as to save on downloading time. Tucows (sorry about the name) have a mirror site at Lancaster University at the following address:

http://micros.hensa.ac.uk/tucows/

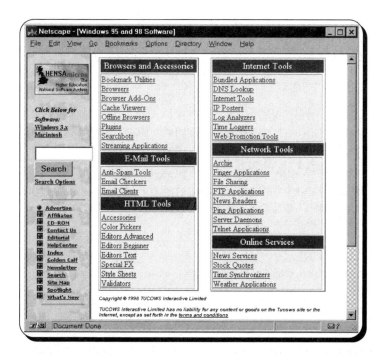

Our screen dump above shows an edited version of some of the software types available when we selected the 'Win 95/98' option from the opening Tucows screen. The HTML Tools section had three pages of Editors. Which one you use is obviously a matter of personal choice, they are all good. The Tucows site ranks all the software on its pages with a 'cow rating' - five cows being the highest! Someone there has a sense of humour.

The editor we use most is HTML Notepad. This is shareware, and is published by Cranial Software who have a Web site at:

http://www.cranial.demon.co.uk

If you want to use it, we will also include it as shareware on the Companion Disc, mentioned on the last page of the book.

19

FTP Programs:

Before we leave the subject of software we will touch on FTP applications, (File Transfer Protocol).

When you create your Web site you will first build it in a folder, or directory, on your PC's hard disc. Once you are happy that everything works and looks 'right', you then have to copy all the files that make up the site to the Web space on your server. From then on, any changes you make to your Web pages will involve changing files on your PC and then copying them around the Internet. This is where FTP comes in. Once a good FTP program is set up, it is simplicity itself to carry out these operations.

There are several FTP programs you can use, but one we like in spite of its name is CuteFTP. To try this out access the following site:

http://cuteftp.com/

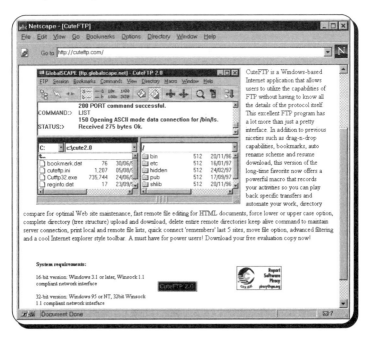

4 - WEB SITE DESIGN

Hopefully now you have all the software you need, or at least know how to access it when you need it. You should be ready to start putting things together and get going on your Web site.

Hiring Someone Else

If the option of learning to build your own pages does not appeal to you, you may wish to hire someone to create the site for you. There are many firms and individuals that offer Web page authoring services (including us), but obviously this will be at a cost. Some will design the page(s) for you; others may simply convert your content and layout into HTML code. How do you go about choosing someone to do it for you? Perhaps the following steps may help.

Spend some time browsing the net, and decide what you like and don't like in Web site design. You could contact sites that you like and ask them to refer you to who built their pages. Or the authors may have a link 'advert' at the bottom of the home pages of their sites.

Then look at an author's previous work by visiting their own site and any others they have built.

Ask previous clients if they were satisfied with the work produced, and the service generally.

Before you make a final choice make sure they have an understanding of how your business can be successful on the Internet and make sure there will be no conflict in styles and personalities.

Payment schemes for the work can come in many varieties: by the hour, per page, per graphic, or per site. A safe way is to agree on what work is to be done, and when and how, and then to negotiate a flat fee. Everyone then knows where they stand.

What makes a well designed web site can be very subjective, and can be very different, depending on who you talk to. We have our own ideas as outlined below, and hope that some of them will be useful to you. If you want a more detailed coverage we suggest the *Guide to Web Style*, produced by Sun Microsystems and located at:

http://www.sun.com/styleguide/tables/Welcome.html

The Importance of Search Engines

To be successful any Web site must be visited and viewed by as many of the people it is designed for as possible. Most people, when they use the Web, use one or more of the Search Engines (see later chapter) to locate sites with the type of content they are interested in at that time. It is critical that this is considered at the outset when you design a site.

You must consider what type of people you want to visit your site and what keywords and phrases they are likely to use when searching for it. There are techniques that any Web site designer should use to maximise the chances of the site being found under relevant search keywords and phrases in the search engines.

These include placing the most important keywords in the TITLE tags of a page, in some of the other META tags available, and then using the main keywords and phrases as many times as possible in the text throughout the rest of your site. The nearer the top of the home page these are, the more likely they are to be picked up in a search. This can often raise problems in a Web site that is composed mainly of graphics.

Make sure your Web designer has experience in this area, or you may want to find one who does.

The Message

Every Web site should have a reason for its existence, whether it is to entertain, to provide information, to display art, or to provide some sort of service such as an index or database. With a commercial organisation it may be to attract new customers and to provide information about products or services. Whatever the reason, it will determine the message the site should be designed to portray.

When most Web users visit a completely new site they only take a few seconds to decide whether to stay and look around, or to surf off somewhere else. A sobering thought, if you are responsible for making them stay.

This really means that the first screen of your opening, or home, page has to load quickly and get over the message you are trying to give. You may not have a second chance.

The important words here are **speed**, **clarity**, **simplicity** and **relevance**. Far too many sites, especially those of large commercial and financial companies, have an enormous graphic image on the opening page, that can take many minutes to download. The decision makers here are obviously not Internet users and don't realise how many people just get fed up waiting and go away. Moral?

If your site is commercial, most of the people who visit it will be there to get some sort of information. They shouldn't be looking for entertainment, or to see the biggest and best logo ever produced. Graphics and special techniques should be used to support and enhance your site, but don't let them overpower its content.

Simplicity

Make sure your Web pages are readable! It's better to have a plain black and white page with no graphics but with very clear text, than to have a page of gimmicky graphics. Make sure your message can be read!

Remember that most browsers can be configured by the user. Such features as non-standard colours and fonts can really mess up a fancy interface. Also be very careful when using graphic images like buttons as link controls. You shouldn't make the user have to guess what to do next. We seem to visit several sites a day where we have to think very hard about what the writer expects us to do. If you do use graphic controls, keep the interface uniform and have the same buttons perform the same actions everywhere on your site.

Backgrounds:

With most browsers now, you have the option of using background colours and images. Be very careful here, it is better to stick with solid light-coloured backgrounds and dark text. Light text on a dark background is harder to read and is much harder on the eye. Obviously, text colour should be the opposite of the background. If the background is light, the text should be dark and if the background is dark, the text should be light.

We like using background images on our sites, but are careful to stick with light pastel coloured embossed 'parchment like' graphics, rather than the multicoloured bright ones seen on many Web sites.

Text:

If you have a lot of text in your pages, give some thought to making it as easy to read as possible. Break up your pages into more easily read chunks, or sections. One page of text that goes on and on scrolling is not a good idea. Only true die-hards will bother reading it. Two screens of information per page is enough in most cases. Try and get the opening page on one screen if you can, and to keep paragraphs to four sentences or less.

Try not to run text the full width of the screen. This creates long lines that are difficult to read. Printed documents have margins, Web pages need them too. There are several ways to do this:

- Using the 'Blockquote' tag, which gives a margin on both sides of the page. These can be nested to vary the width as necessary.

- Our favourite way is to use nested tables to control the overall page layout.

- You can also use lists as a simple way of formatting text that requires indentation.

Consider Colour Carefully:

Colour is visually very important to most people. Try not to overdo its use, but use it to draw attention where it's really needed. Web browsers use this principle by displaying a page's links in colours that stand out from the rest of the text. By default, two different colours are used to show which links have been visited and which haven't.

In fact many people seem to scan Web pages reading only the link text and not the main body at all. It is a good idea to leave the text and links in their default colours so that your visitors will find it much easier to navigate around your site.

Different Web Browsers:

One problem with Web site design is that different browsers can treat your code in different ways. It seems to us that the more modern the browser software is, the less standard it will be. It does not make sense to build your site for one type of browser. At the moment the people who visit our sites seem to be equally split between Netscape and Microsoft Explorer users and only a relatively small percentage use the latest version numbers. With this in mind, be careful about using the latest features that only a few will be able to take advantage of. In this book we will restrict ourselves to fairly basic HTML design features. The more basic your code, the more likely it is that most people's browsers will render it the way you intend.

As graphics take time to download many people surf the Web with the graphics turned off in their browsers. You should always think about what your site will look like without its graphics. Can people still get your site's message, or will all the formatting and logic disappear?

Another problem area may soon be the extensive use of browsers built into add-ons to TV, or other, sets. These may well be very basic and much more like older versions of the present browsers.

What we are trying to say here is to assume that your users will have only a basic browser, therefore build your site accordingly. Simplicity does not mean it has to be boring though, just better designed!

The Use of Graphics

The loading speed of your Web pages will largely be determined by your use of graphics. Video and sound files will obviously also slow your site down, but we do not use either of these at all, so will not be spending any more time on them. If your site relies on the latest pop music or excerpts from a movie you may obviously feel very different!

When designing your Web pages, you need to keep in mind that people will be downloading them, sometimes with slow modems. This means they'll have to wait for every image to download, which can take a long time. You should limit the number of images on a page and make sure they are made as small as possible, both in size on the page and in file size. Every image you put on a page should be vital to the topic of the page, not be there just to look good. Unnecessary images only slow down the loading of your web pages.

Using Thumbnail Images:

The physical size of a graphic when it appears on the screen has a direct correlation with the size of the file that has to be fetched. The larger the image, the larger the file size, and the longer it takes to download.

When you have large images that are necessary to your site, simply produce thumbnails of them (very much smaller versions), and put the thumbnail on your page, with a link so that when it is clicked the larger version can be viewed. This way only the people that are interested in seeing the full size version need sit through the time it takes to download. It is a good idea when you do this, to put text alongside the thumbnail to tell the reader how big the file is, to give them an idea of how long they'll have to wait.

Creating thumbnails just means reducing the dimensions of your image and saving it under a new name. To do this you will need image editing software such as Adobe Photoshop, Corel Photo-Paint or the excellent graphics package Paint Shop Pro. A fully functional trial version of the latter program can be downloaded from the publisher's Web site at:

http://www.jasc.com

If you have Windows 98, you could also use the updated Paint program that comes with it. This now supports the Internet file formats .JPG and .GIF.

If you have installed Microsoft Office from a CD-ROM, you may have a version of Photo Editor on your PC, or it may be on the CD-ROM. Have a look for it, because this small program will also manipulate graphic images and may be all you need.

Minimising the File Size of Graphics:

At the present time on the Internet there are two main graphic image formats to use, GIF and JPEG (JPG).

The GIF format is generally best for non-photo graphics, such as clip art. When a file is saved in this format the image is compressed as much as possible without 'dropping out' any data. So GIF images retain their quality, at the expense of usually larger file sizes. One other advantage of the GIF format is that you can set the image's background to be transparent, which can make your graphics look more interesting on the page.

The JPEG format is best used for photographic images only, as it compresses the image, making the file size smaller, by dropping out bits of the image, and photos usually show less degradation of quality. If you are saving an image as a JPEG, you can control the amount of compression you wish to use. The higher the compression, the lower the quality will be and the smaller the file size. There are two ways to reduce the file size of your images without reducing their physical size.

When saving a file as a JPEG you can control the resolution the file will display in dots per inch (DPI). If a file is to be printed, a high value is needed of 300 or more, but if it is to be just displayed on a computer screen, as on a Web page, 75 DPI is fine. As most files are scanned at a high resolution you can usually reduce the file size dramatically this way. We find that a Compression Level of 70 also gives a good compromise between file size and quality. Some purists, however, will never use JPEG files because of the reduction in image quality. Life is all about compromise!

If necessary, you can also shrink the size of the image file by reducing the number of colours in the image. Most scanned photographs will be in 'True Colour' and be made up of many thousands of different colours. Many people browsing the web will have their systems set for only 256 colours. For them anything over that is a waste. If you reduce your image's colours to 256 you may well not notice the difference, except in the file size!

Interlaced Graphics:

The latest version of the GIF format, GIF89a, can save graphics as interlaced files. This means that rather than saving the image line by line from the top to the bottom, every fifth line is first saved and the next lines down are added on four subsequent passes, until the whole image is saved. With a modern browser this type of image will load very quickly from top to bottom with an initial low quality which will gradually sharpen as the infill lines are loaded. Users do not have to wait for the whole image to load before they can see what it is and decide whether or not they want to wait any longer.

Navigation Round the Site

A Web site is usually made up with a home, or index, page which (hopefully) opens first, and other linked pages containing the site data, as shown below.

Before starting to design your site give a lot of thought to its 'roadmap', to how its different elements will be linked together, and how this navigational information will be conveyed to the user. In our example on the next page the links shown only go in one direction. Is this a good idea? In fact with this set-up you couldn't visit the whole site without using the Back button on your browser.

You may have definite ideas about how you want people to travel through your site, in which case organise the links on each page to steer them that way. But beware, many like to do their own thing, so you really ought to cater for them as well. We like to put clear text links, located towards the top of the home

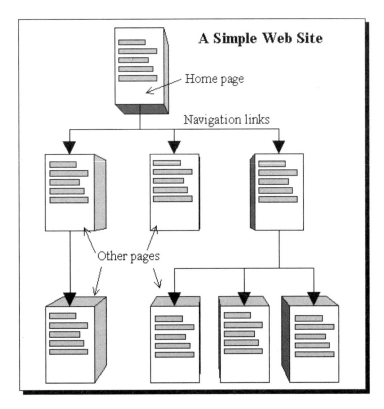

A Simple Web Site

Home page

Navigation links

Other pages

page, to all the main areas of the site. That way people can see immediately what is on offer.

One problem to watch for is that search engines can direct people to any of the pages on your site, so you should look at every page as a potential starting point. A link to the home, or index, page is a good idea on every page of the site. For the same reason, it is not wise to use links called 'Return' or 'Back', because there is no guarantee where they came from! Much better to name your links with a clear phrase or expression that describes the destination.

For pages longer than the screen, it is worth repeating any navigational links at the bottom of a page as well as having them at the top. Also with a long page we like to see a link to the top that shows on every screen of data. This helps your users keep their orientation. Don't forget to make it easy for a visitor to determine what is new on your site and when things were changed.

When reviewing the design of your site, some questions to ask yourself might be:

- Could someone, after visiting my site, draw a simple diagram showing how the different elements are connected and how you get from one place to another? If not, why not?

- How easy is it to locate specific information on the site?

- How does a visitor figure out all of the things they can see or do at the site, and tell if they have seen everything?

One last thought before we leave this section is that a site that is difficult to navigate will probably also be difficult to maintain and keep up to date. Don't make a rod for your own back!

Tables and Frames

Most modern browsers are capable of using frames, which can split a page into rectangular areas, each one being capable of displaying its own Web page. The use of frames is controlled by the page author using HTML. Each frame can contain scroll bars to let you view more information.

As some browsers do not handle frames you should be careful if you use them, and provide alternative non-frame code. That way everyone will be able to access your pages in their own way. We will not be spending much time in this book on frames.

Tables:

Tables are a very different matter. They have two main uses. The first for presenting information you want to display in a grid, like in a spreadsheet. But, much more useful, you can also use tables to give greater control over your Web page layout. One problem with building pages is that HTML does not give you much control over the display of your work. When first used this was intentional. Most data was text based and the HTML tags were designed to give browsers an idea of the type and importance of the data in each paragraph. The browser itself then formatted each paragraph to fit the available screen space.

Once you start embedding graphics in the text and try to create other visually pleasing effects this can lead to serious problems. Especially as users have different resolution monitors which can display your Web pages with different viewing widths.

The easiest way round this is to use tables in your pages to control their display. We are told that most people use a 14" monitor, set to a display resolution of 640 pixels wide by 480 pixels high. In many cases then, it will pay to limit the width of your Web page content to fit this screen. This is easy to do by designing the whole page inside a table with a width of 600 pixels. The table border should usually be set to 0, in which case it will be invisible. It is also possible to nest tables within each other. In this way you can break the page up into areas containing the different text and graphic elements of the display.

Print Output

When we find a Web page with content worth keeping, the first thing we usually do is print it out onto paper. If you have tried this you will know that the results are often 'catastrophic'. You should always ask yourself what the pages of your site look like when printed.

If you have a lot of browser-specific code, such as textured or graphic backgrounds and animated banners or graphics, they may not print as you expect. In fact they often throw the whole output out of line, or with some sections overprinting others.

Frames often don't print correctly. But the worst effects are often from pages which have black or dark backgrounds and white or light-coloured text.

Think about Maintenance

Everything changes in life, the Web changes, and pretty soon your brand new site will need updating. This is called maintenance, and it can be a pain. Another reason for keeping your site right up to date, is to encourage people to visit it. If a site has not changed for many months the search engines seem to lose interest in it and it slowly slides down the search rankings.

You can design your site to make it easier to modify. It helps to use systematic formatting of your HTML code, and not link everything on the site with everything else. HTML documents that are easy to read are easier to maintain. Use blank lines and spaces to separate elements, and be consistent.

One thing that makes sense is to create a set of uniform formats and styles for your pages. This gives your site a 'complete' style and helps your readers to find their way round it. It also means you can create a new page by copying and modifying an existing page.

If you have links to other sites you must keep them up-to-date and accurate. This means checking them on a regular basis. You will find that sites move around on the Internet, as they grow out of the space allocated to them, or they 'fall out' with their hosts. Some of your links will need regularly altering to save your readers the frustration of a succession of 'site not found' type messages.

5. USING A WYSIWYG EDITOR

As an example of how easy it can be to build quite presentable Web pages we will step you through the process. In this chapter we use the WYSIWYG (what you see is what you get) editor, called Composer, that is built into the Netscape Communicator browser. If you don't want to use this, you can use one of the top range versions of the Word or WordPro word processors, to do virtually the same thing. But maybe not quite as well, or as easily! For the rest of this chapter we assume you have a version of Netscape Communicator 4 (or above) set up on your PC, which can be obtained free of charge as described on page 18.

Getting Started

The sample small site we will construct is based on one of our actual Web sites, that was built for the artist Michael Strang. You can access this with the following URL address:

http://www.michaelstrang.com

Most of the pages on the actual site contain code for tracking visitors (which we do not want to cover here), so we have used the **tutorial** folder to work from. All the files you need for our example are stored there, and we will tell you how to extract them now.

Your Working Folder:

As we mentioned earlier, you first build your Web site on your own PC, and only when it is finished do you place it on your server. For our example you will need to create a working folder (or directory) to hold all the files. What you call it is up to you, but ours goes by the name of Website, and is located on our D: drive. Hence the path on our PC is D:\Website\, and its initial contents are shown on the next page.

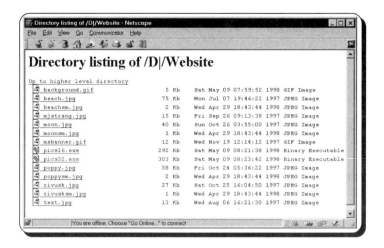

Directory listing of /D|/Website

```
Up to higher level directory
  background.gif          5 Kb    Sat May 09 07:59:52 1998 GIF Image
  beach.jpg              75 Kb    Mon Jul 07 19:46:22 1997 JPEG Image
  beachsm.jpg             2 Kb    Wed Apr 29 18:43:44 1998 JPEG Image
  mjstrang.jpg           15 Kb    Fri Sep 26 09:13:38 1997 JPEG Image
  moon.jpg               40 Kb    Sun Oct 26 03:55:00 1997 JPEG Image
  moonsm.jpg              1 Kb    Wed Apr 29 18:43:44 1998 JPEG Image
  msbanner.gif           12 Kb    Wed Nov 19 12:14:12 1997 GIF Image
  pics16.exe            292 Kb    Sat May 09 08:21:38 1998 Binary Executable
  pics32.exe            303 Kb    Sat May 09 08:23:42 1998 Binary Executable
  poppy.jpg              58 Kb    Fri Oct 24 05:36:22 1997 JPEG Image
  poppysm.jpg             2 Kb    Wed Apr 29 18:43:44 1998 JPEG Image
  rivusk.jpg             27 Kb    Sat Oct 25 16:04:50 1997 JPEG Image
  rivusksm.jpg            1 Kb    Wed Apr 29 18:43:44 1998 JPEG Image
  text.jpg               13 Kb    Wed Aug 06 16:21:30 1997 JPEG Image
```

You are offline. Choose "Go Online..." to connect

Getting the Picture Files:

As the Web pages you are going to produce are about
an artist, you will need some graphic images of his
work. The easiest way for you to get these is by
downloading them from our site. If you are using
Windows 95, 98 or NT, type the following URL address
into the Location window of your browser:

http://www.michaelstrang.com/tutorial/pics32.exe

If you are using an older version of Windows use the
following:

http://www.michaelstrang.com/tutorial/pics16.exe

In either case, save the file to your work folder when
asked for a location. These are both 'self extracting'
files and simply double clicking on them in a File
window will start the process of extracting the files to
your hard disc.

If you are not connected to the Internet, or don't want
to download them, you can also get them from the
Companion Disc that you can obtain for this book (see
the last page for details).

The Netscape Composer

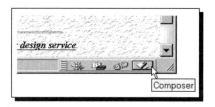

Now we are finally
ready to begin. With
the Communicator
running, open a
Composer window by
clicking the icon in
the bottom right-hand
corner, shown here.
Alternatively you could use the **File**, **New**, **Blank Page**
menu command, or the <Ctrl+Shift+N> keyboard
shortcut. All of these methods open an empty and
untitled window, like that shown below, for you to start
building in.

The Composer has two toolbars to quickly action the
more common authoring commands. Moving the
mouse pointer over an icon 'lights it up', and opens a
small banner which describes the function of the icon.
A more detailed description is shown on the status bar,
but for easy reference we have also included the
toolbar functions on the next page. Some can also be
actioned by using a keyboard shortcut (such as
<Ctrl+B> for Bold). Where applicable we have included
these.

The Composition Toolbar:

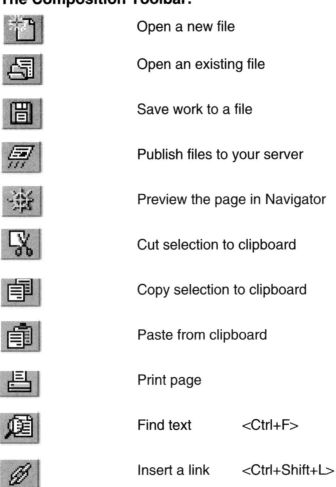

Open a new file

Open an existing file

Save work to a file

Publish files to your server

Preview the page in Navigator

Cut selection to clipboard

Copy selection to clipboard

Paste from clipboard

Print page

Find text   \<Ctrl+F\>

Insert a link   \<Ctrl+Shift+L\>

Insert target

Insert image

Insert a full width horizontal line

 Insert a table

 Check spelling of page

The Formatting Toolbar:

 Change paragraph style

 Change font

 Font size

 Font colour

 Bold   <Ctrl+B>

 Italic   <Ctrl+I>

A Underline   <Ctrl+U>

Remove styles   <Ctrl+K>

Bullet list

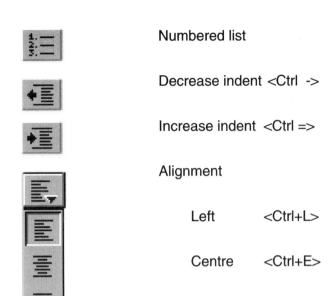

Numbered list

Decrease indent <Ctrl ->

Increase indent <Ctrl =>

Alignment

Left   <Ctrl+L>

Centre   <Ctrl+E>

Right   <Ctrl+R>

Using Composer Help:

Unlike earlier versions of Netscape, Communicator 4 comes with a very complete help system built in. Before going too much further it would be as well to explore this.

The **Help**, **Help Contents** menu command opens the help window for the whole Communicator suite. Selecting the **About Composer** option in the left column and then clicking the **Using Composer** link which is located after the general description of the program, will open the material shown on the next page.

This Help information is so good we will leave it to you to go through it, and will certainly not attempt to duplicate it.

Our First Web Page

When you have finished with the Help page, return to an empty Composer window and type the following two paragraphs of text:

MICHAEL STRANG

Michael Strang, the contemporary British artist who lives in Cornwall, specialises in textured oil paintings of seascapes, landscapes and flowers - especially poppies.

Centre each of the paragraphs by placing the cursor in it and using the Centre Alignment icon, or the <Ctrl+E> short cut.

We will now set the font sizes of the text. The default settings offered by the Font Size icon are in point sizes. As you do not know what settings your reader's browsers will have it is better to always use relative sizes. That way your page text will always look relatively bigger or smaller than the browser default.

To change this setting, use the **Edit**, **Preferences** menu command and on the Composer settings page set the **Font Size Mode** to **Show relative HTML font scale...** and press **OK**.

When next you use the Font Size icon it will look like that shown here. A font size set at 0 will display as the browser default, the +ve sizes will display larger than this in steps, and the −ve ones will display at smaller sizes.

Formatting Text:

We can now use the toolbars to format the text just like in a word processor. First select paragraph one by moving the pointer to its left end and clicking when it becomes an arrow, as shown here. Select

Heading 3 from the Paragraph Style icon and then click the Font Colour icon. This will open a palette of colours for you to choose from, as shown here to the left.

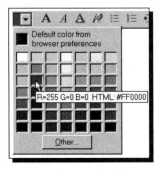

We want red, which when the pointer is passed over it shows as Hex FF0000, the format used in HTML, or with its RGB properties. For our purposes here simply Red is good enough! If you click the **Other** button, you can choose from a much bigger palette, or customise colours of your own.

Now make sure the font size of the second paragraph is the default value, 0 before we save our work so far.

Saving a Page File:

It always pays to save your work often when using a computer. Power cuts do not seem as common as they once were, but they still happen. Losing ten minutes effort is a nuisance, but losing a day's work is a catastrophe.

Clicking the Save icon will open the **Save As** box if a page has not been previously saved. Select your working folder, type

index

in the **File name** box and click the **Save** button. This does not save the file straight away but asks for a Title for the Web page you are creating.

This title is the text that will appear in the Title bar of your page and is important as it controls how the page will be handled by search engines. It needs to describe the site and contain the most important search keywords, but also be concise and fit into the space, as shown below.

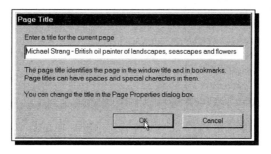

Once you have entered the title text, clicking OK will complete the file saving operation. This is a once only procedure, the next time you click the Save icon, the file will be automatically saved in the background.

Your Composer window should now look something like ours shown at the top on the next page. Note the title bar has changed somewhat.

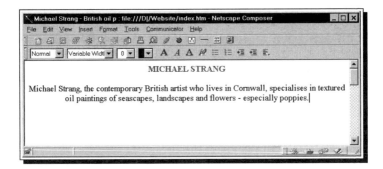

Previewing the Page:

 Before we go any further, let's see what our text looks like in the browser. This is easy to do, simply clicking the Preview in Navigator icon opens a new window in Navigator with your page displayed, as shown below.

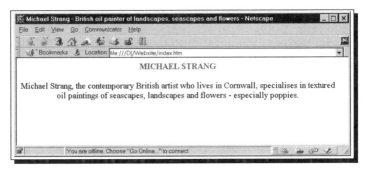

There is not very much difference between the two views of our page, which demonstrates that working in the WYSIWYG mode gives you a good view of what you can expect to see in your browser. Sometimes, though, you need to move between the two modes quite often to get the visual effect you are looking for.

In the views above the first paragraph text does not stand out enough, so in the Composer window, set its font size to +2. Saving the file again and pressing the Reload icon in the Navigator window will let you see the effects of the change straight away.

Adding Graphics to the Page:

Now we will give our page some visual impact by adding some graphics. With the cursor, or insertion point, located at the end of the second paragraph press <Shift+Enter> to insert a new line break. Click the Centre Alignment icon followed by the Insert Image icon. This opens the Image Properties dialogue box shown here.

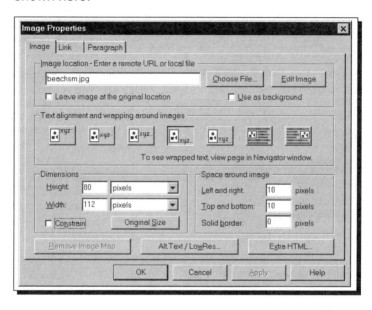

Fill this box in as shown. First click **Choose File** and select beachsm.jpg (the thumbnail image of beach.jpg) from your working folder.

Set the image **Height** to 80 pixels, and with the **Constrain** box unselected, set the image **Width** to 112 pixels. Then set the **Space around image** to 10 pixels **Left and Right** and 10 pixels **Top and Bottom**. These sizes and spaces are needed as we will have a block of four images of the same size together on our page.

Click the **Alt. Text/Low Res** button to enter the text that will show 'behind' the image, as follows.

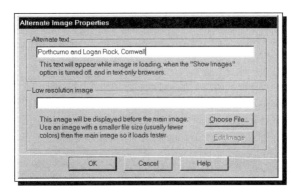

We will not bother with a low resolution image as ours is very small and fast loading already. Press **OK** to return to the main dialogue box and click the **Link** tab. It is here that you control what image or page is opened when the thumbnail is clicked on your Web page.

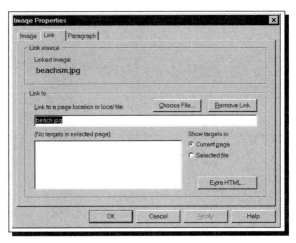

Type beach.jpg in the **Link to page location or local file** box, as shown above. You could, of course, have used the **Choose File** button and selected the file visually, but you would then have to have set the **Files of type** setting to **All files (*.*)**.

Clicking **OK** will close the Image Properties box and return you to the Composer window. Hopefully this should have the thumbnail image as shown below. Note that the 'Alt' (for alternative) text that you entered is displayed when you pass the pointer over the image. The link address that was placed should also show on the Status bar at the same time.

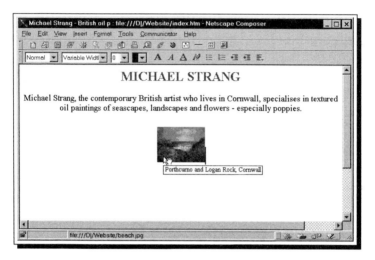

Save the file and press the Reload icon in the Navigator window, as before, to make sure everything works. Clicking on the thumbnail should display the full image in the window, but you will then have to press the Back icon to return to your main page.

If all is well so far, you can add the other three thumbnail images, if not, make yourself a cup of coffee, and try and work out what went wrong!

In the Composer window you can check and edit any of the settings of a placed image by right-clicking on it and choosing **Image / Link Properties** from the 'pop-up' context menu. Be careful though as the program has a way of then choosing some default settings that you may not want, and it can also add unwanted paths to a file address.

47

The Other Images:

To place the other three thumbnail images, make sure you have the Composer window active and that the insertion point (a flashing vertical bar) is immediately to the right of the first image. If not use the keyboard direction arrows to move it there, and then click the Insert Image icon.

Fill in the dialogue boxes as before with the same size and spaces settings, but with the following data in the other boxes.

Thumbnail 2
Image name - poppysm.jpg
Linked to - poppy.jpg
Alternative text - Poppies on the edge of a Cornish cornfield

Thumbnail 3
Image name - moonsm.jpg
Linked to - moon.jpg
Alternative text - Gulval Sunflowers by Moonlight, Cornwall

Thumbnail 4
Image name - rivusksm.jpg
Linked to - rivusk.jpg
Alternative text - On the River Usk, Near Tallybont, South Wales

The second two images should be on a new line so press the <Enter> key before placing thumbnail 3. Press it again after the last one, and the block of images should be complete.

If any of the images has a coloured frame round it check that **Solid border** (in the **Space around image** section) is set to 0 pixels. The border, if left, will change colour to show that a link has been followed, but this feature spoils the graphic effects of most layouts, so is rarely used for images.

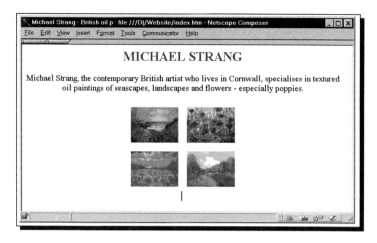

Our page at this stage is shown above in the Composer window.

Image Properties:

Before we go any further a few comments are needed about the image properties we have just seen, and the importance of their use.

Giving details of the height and width of an image allows the browser receiving a Web page to immediately allocate space for the image on the page. This both speeds up the process and allows the page layout to be more correctly formed from the start, as shown here.

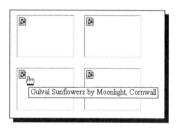

Some people surf the Net with graphics turned off on their browsers, and indeed some still use browsers that do not display graphics. If you do not dimension your images and use Alternative text, these people will have no idea what your Web pages are about. The Alternative text is useful even when a browser does display graphics as it usually displays inside the image outline while the graphic file is being downloaded. This gives the user an idea of the likely page contents at a very early stage. Alternative text also displays as banners when you pass the pointer over an image with the most recent browsers, as shown in our example on the previous page.

The Remaining Text:

There is not much more to this page now. Action the **Insert**, **Break below Image(s)** menu command and then simply type the text as it appears below.

The <Enter> key can be used once to start a new line, but if you need to force more space you have to use the <Shift+Enter> keyboard command.

To place the line, click the Insert Horizontal Line icon. In our case we don't want it to be full screen width so right-click the pointer on the line and select **Horizontal Line Properties** from the pop-up menu.

This allows you to set the line's **Height** (or thickness), its **Width** relative to the page, its alignment and whether it is given a shadow, as chosen here, by checking the **3-D shading** box.

To insert the copyright symbol (©), open the Windows Character Map application from the Start Menu bar, set the font to Times New Roman, copy the symbol to the clipboard and then paste it into the Composer window.

The Menu line should be Font Size +1, the others Size -1 and the last line should be set to the Paragraph Style of Address.

Creating Text Links:

We have already seen how easy it is to create links to other pages and files from a graphic image, now it is time to create some text links. The menu on our page is a text based one, and each item on it must be linked to another Web page. The first items 'About the Artist' and 'Gallery' will link to pages in our tutorial site that are not yet created, so although we will place the links now they will not actually work yet. The other item will link to the home page on the actual Strang site.

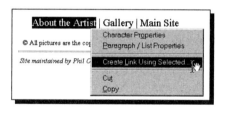

Highlight the first menu item text, as shown here, right-click the pointer and select **Create Link using** **Selected..** from the pop-up menu. Then type the future page name *artist.htm* in the **Link to a page location or local file** text box, and press the **OK** button. In the same way link 'Gallery' to the page *gallery.htm* and 'Main Site' to the URL

http://www.michaelstrang.com

All three menu links are now placed and the menu items should have changed to a bright blue colour and be underlined.

A Mailto Link:

We have one more link to place yet, but this is a special one. It is considered good practice to 'sign' your Web pages at the bottom and provide an e-mail address so that your readers know where the page originated and can contact you if they need to.

This is very easily done by creating a link with your e-mail address preceded by the expression 'mailto:'. To do this in our example we created the statement

mailto:prmolive@csm.ex.ac.uk

which was linked to the page author's name (Phil Oliver) in the last line of text, as can be seen on the status bar of the example below.

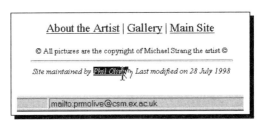

When the link is clicked in the browser window the user's default e-mail program is activated and a new message window is opened already addressed to the page author. Try it, it is quite neat, and works for most browsers. In fact with Netscape you can also control the Subject of the e-mail, but this does not seem to work with all Microsoft browsers, so we will not bother with it here.

The Body of the page (the part you can see in your browser) is now complete; we still have the Head section to complete.

Setting Page Properties

Useful information about your Web page can be placed in the Head section which can both help the search engines find your page in the first place, and then, to some extent, can control what information is displayed in their search results. With your page open in a Composer window, use the **F̲ormat**, **Page Colors and Properties** menu command to open the dialogue box shown below, with the General tab selected.

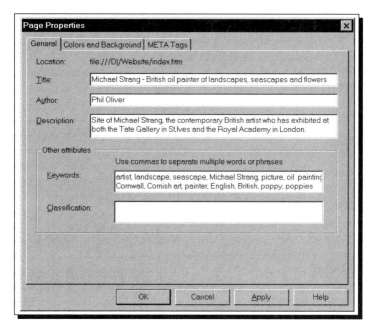

The **T̲itle** property we have seen before, but you can change or edit it here. This gives the text you want to appear in the window title bar when the document is browsed. This is how many Web search tools locate specific Web pages, so if you want readers to be able to locate your page easily, select a useful title that conveys what your page is all about.

Author - The name of the person who created the page.

Description - A few words describing the contents of the page. This is usually the information that readers are given about the page when a search tool, or engine, locates it in a search for a specific topic.

Keywords - Enter here the words and combinations of words that you want the search to use when locating your site on the Web.

What you place in these boxes is critical to how successful your Web site will be. There are millions of Web pages available for users to find, so you have to help the search engines both to locate your site and then to present it so that people will want to select it from a long list of alternative choices.

Page Colours:

When you have completed the entries on the previous 'General' tab sheet, click the 'Colors and Background' tab to open the following box.

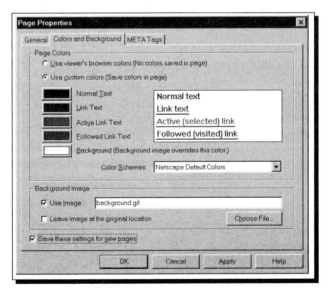

In this dialogue box you can control the text and link colours of your page as well as the background.

We prefer to keep Netscape's default text and link colours on our sites, and to force this by saving the settings with the page. By tradition most surfers expect unused text links to be a bright blue colour and visited ones to be a dark mauve. Why change this, just for the sake of it.

To do this, select **Use custom colors (Save colors in page)** and make sure that 'Netscape Default Colors' is selected in the **Color Schemes** drop down list. This will embed code on your page that will override a viewer's browser settings and hopefully force the correct display of your text. If you don't do this and a browser has non-standard viewing settings your page may be unreadable. Be warned, it is a mistake we have made.

Page Background:

The default page background colour for Netscape 4 is white, some browsers default to a grey background. You can however control this by selecting any colour in the **Background (Background image overrides this colour)** option of the previous dialogue box.

We want to control our page background even further, so have selected the **Use Image** option in the Background Image section. The file *background.gif* contains an off-white parchment textured image, which we think gives a pleasing background for our type of site. If you are building this, or a similar, site as you read this, the file will be in the batch you downloaded (see page 36).

Click **OK** to make the changes you have made effective and close the dialogue box. Alternatively you could click **Apply** to preview the changes and then click **Close** to accept them and exit the box.

The home, or opening, page of our small tutorial site is now finished. To see what it looks like, click the Preview in Navigator button shown here, and select **Yes** to first save the page. Our page is shown below for comparison.

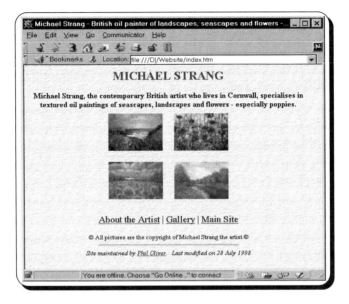

6. AN OVERVIEW OF HTML

As we saw in an earlier chapter, HTML stands for HyperText Markup Language, and consists of a series of style markings, called markup tags, which control the data to be displayed in an ASCII or text file. These 'tags' determine how a browser displays the data when the Web page is viewed. On the whole they are independent of the 'platform' used, a page looking pretty much the same in a UNIX, Macintosh or a Windows environment.

It is certainly possible to build and manage Web sites without knowing much HTML, but it is not a difficult discipline to learn. With it you can 'fine tune' your pages to get much better visual display. We cover here a brief introduction to get you started.

Introduction to HTML

An easy way to view some HTML is to look at the source code of a Web page in your browser. The example below shows part of the code for the page *index.htm* developed in the last chapter.

57

In our version of Netscape Navigator this was obtained by using the **View**, **Page Source** menu command (or the <Ctrl+U> keystroke shortcut) with the page active in the browser. This lets you look at the source code, but not alter it in any way. We will look at this code in a little more detail later in the chapter.

A better way to 'play with' the code of any page you are viewing with your browser is to save the file to your PC with the **File**, **Save As** <Ctrl+S> command. Make sure you set the **Save as type** to HTML Files though, or the saved file will have all the HTML tags stripped from it! You can then open the saved file in any text editor such as Notepad, or an HTML editor. Looking at other people's code is a very good way to learn how they achieved the effects on their Web pages. This does not, however, always work very well if the viewed Web page is designed with frames.

Some Background

The name of an HTML file always ends with the extension '.htm' or on some systems '.html' to identify its type.

As with everything else in the computer world things develop at a rapid pace, and there are many versions and 'flavours' of HTML. As more complex new browsers come out, both Microsoft and Netscape have added new features to the language. All of the HTML we cover here is fairly standard and should work with most browsers that are around.

HTML documents are free-format, you can use spaces and tabs anywhere you like in them, and break lines anywhere. Only one 'space' character will be recognised in text, any more will be ignored. So white space and line breaks will not affect the document appearance in a browser except when used inside certain special tags which we describe later.

With this in mind, you can make your HTML pages much easier to read by spreading out the code and arranging it in a systematic way. Unfortunately the code produced by Netscape Composer does not always fall into this category, as you can see by looking at our example!

HTML is not case sensitive, so you can use upper or lower case text in your tags, or a mixture of both. For example <HEAD> is the same as <head> or <Head>. A good convention is to use upper case for the tags and lower case for any other text entered.

Elements, Tags and Attributes:

An element is a basic component of the structure of a text document, such as head, body, table, paragraph, and list. Elements can contain plain text, other elements, or both.

HTML tags are used to mark the elements of a file for your browser. Tags begin with a left-angle bracket < and end with a right-angle bracket >. The first text between the angle brackets is the name of the tag. For example:

   <H2>

is the opening tag for a heading element.

Any further words and characters in a tag are the attributes, e.g. align=center in the example below.

   <H2 ALIGN="CENTER"> This is a Heading </H2>

This is a complete instruction, which tells the browser reading it to format the text 'This is a Heading' as a second level heading, centred on the page.

A tag is therefore the basic 'instruction', and an attribute is some extra detail such as how to align the text. Most tags possess 'closing tags' such as </H2>, above, which mark the place where the effect of the tag should stop.

Document Structure

An HTML document consists of two main parts, the Head, and the Body. The basic document structure is:

```
<HTML>
<HEAD> ... </HEAD>
<BODY> ... </BODY>
</HTML>
```

The HEAD contains information about the document, and the BODY contains the document data to be displayed.

The HEAD Element:

The head element contains all the information about the document, such as the <TITLE> or <META> information. It does not contain any text which is part of the document, this should be in the <BODY>. The <HEAD> would follow the <HTML> tag and precede the <BODY> element.

The contents of the document <HEAD> is an unordered collection of the following elements:

TITLE   defines the document title, and is always needed.

ISINDEX   for simple keyword searches.

BASE   defines base URL for resolving relative URLs.

SCRIPT   reserved for use with scripting languages.

STYLE   reserved for use with style sheets.

META   used to supply meta info as name/value pairs.

LINK   used to define relationships with other documents.

The only two of these we will worry about here are TITLE and META.

Every document should have a title - it appears as a page title on the browser window, and when a user bookmarks it, looks in their history list, or receives information from a search engine. Take care to keep the title short, but make it a good meaningful one. "My home page" is not much help to another user!

Take a look below at a slightly edited version of the more important HEAD elements of our example Web site home page, from the last chapter.

```
<HEAD>

<META NAME="Author" CONTENT="Phil Oliver">

<META NAME="Generator" CONTENT="Mozilla/4.04 [en]
(Win95; I) [Netscape]">

<TITLE>Michael Strang - British oil painter of landscapes,
seascapes and flowers</TITLE>

<META NAME="Description" CONTENT="Site of Michael
Strang, the contemporary British artist who has exhibited
at both the Tate Gallery in St.Ives and the Royal Academy in
London.">

<META NAME="KeyWords" CONTENT="artist, landscape,
seascape, Michael Strang, picture, oil painting, Cornwall,
Cornish art, painter, English, British, poppy, poppies">

</HEAD>
```

This illustrates the use of the META expressions.

Don't panic now, it is not necessary to learn these, you can include them in a template to use for your new pages. Once you understand what each one does, it is simple to add the text in the CONTENT="xxx" section that is relevant to the page you are working on.

"Author" and **"Generator"** give information on whose page it is and what software they used to generate it. No problems at all if you leave these out.

"Description" gives a few words describing the contents of the page. This is usually the information that readers are given about the page when a search tool, or engine, locates it in a search for a specific topic.

"Keywords" should list the words and combinations of words that you want the search to use when locating your site on the Web.

What you place in these boxes is critical to how successful your Web site will be. As we have mentioned previously, there are millions of Web pages available to users, so you have to help the search engines to locate and present your site so that people will want to select it from a long list of alternative choices.

The BODY Element:

As we saw earlier, the document to be displayed is placed between the BODY opening and closing tags.

The opening BODY element tag itself is used to hold the attributes that control the background and foreground colours for normal text and hypertext links and a background image for the whole page, for example,

```
<BODY TEXT="#000000" BGCOLOR="#FFFFFF"
LINK="#0000FF" VLINK="#800080" ALINK="#FF0000"
BACKGROUND="bg.gif">
```

BGCOLOR   Specifies the background colour for the document body.

TEXT   Specifies the colour used for the document's text.

LINK	Specifies the colour used for the text of unvisited hypertext links.
VLINK	Specifies the colour used for the text of visited hypertext links.
ALINK	Specifies the highlight colour used for the text of links at the moment the user clicks on them.
BACKGROUND	Specifies a URL for an image to be used to tile the document background.

In HTML, colours are given as hexadecimal numbers (e.g. COLOR="#C0FFC0") as in the previous example, or as one of a list of widely understood colour names, as in the example below.

**<BODY TEXT=black BGCOLOR=white LINK=blue
VLINK=purple ALINK=red BACKGROUND=file.gif>**

The most common colour 'names' used are shown below, which were originally picked as being the standard 16 colours supported with the Windows VGA palette. Some browsers recognise many others, but most will be happy with these.

Black	= "#000000"	Green	= "#008000"
Silver	= "#C0C0C0"	Lime	= "#00FF00"
Grey	= "#808080"	Olive	= "#808000"
White	= "#FFFFFF"	Yellow	= "#FFFF00"
Maroon	= "#800000"	Navy	= "#000080"
Red	= "#FF0000"	Blue	= "#0000FF"
Purple	= "#800080"	Teal	= "#008080"
Fuchsia	= "#FF00FF"	Aqua	= "#00FFFF"

Don't forget that when coding you have to use the American spelling of words such as 'color' and 'center'.

The Basic HTML Elements

These are the main HTML elements that appear in the body of a document, or page. Some of them also cause a paragraph break.

Headings:

We saw an example of a heading several pages back.

<H2 ALIGN="CENTER"> This is a Heading </H2>

Heading text is displayed in larger and/or bolder fonts than normal body text. There are six headings: H1, H2, H3, H4, H5, and H6. H1 is the "main" heading, usually used once at the top of the document. H6 is the "smallest" header and is rarely used.

It is considered bad practice to skip levels of headings in your document. Headings not only give some format and 'importance' to title lines of text, but can be used by some software to generate outlines of your document, or tables of contents. Search engines also seem to attach more importance to words depending on their position in the heading hierarchy.

Line Breaks:

As mentioned before, white space and line breaks are ignored by Web browsers except inside special tags. You have to provide tags to indicate them. If you want to force a line break use the <BR> tag.

The CLEAR attribute can be used inside this tag to move down past floating images on either margin.

<BR CLEAR=LEFT>   Moves down past floating images on the left margin.

<BR CLEAR=RIGHT>   Does the same for those on the right margin.

<BR CLEAR=ALL>   Moves the entry point below all images.

Paragraphs:

If you want a paragraph break - a line break with an empty line between paragraphs - use the tag

   <P>

This element is a container and requires a start tag. The end tag </P> is optional as it can be inferred by the browser which should place paragraph breaks before and after <P> elements.

   Text within a paragraph is generally wrapped to fit the space available and is usually rendered flush left with a ragged right margin. The ALIGN attribute can be used inside the <P> tag to control the alignment:

   ALIGN=LEFT   Paragraph text flush left.

   ALIGN=CENTER Paragraph is centred.

   ALIGN=RIGHT   Paragraph text flush right.

   ALIGN=JUSTIFY Paragraph text flush to both left and right edges, with the spacing between words being varied. This is only available on the latest browsers. Otherwise it is ignored.

Links and Anchor Tags:

The fundamental feature of the Web that makes it so powerful is of course, hypertext links. The tag that creates these links is called the anchor tag (A). The most commonly used attribute: HREF, specifies the URL of the target document, e.g..

   <A HREF="page02.htm">Next page</A>

This links the text 'Next page' to the HTML document *page02.htm*. When the linked text is clicked, the other document will be opened in the browser.

If a *.jpg*, or *.gif*, file is linked as shown below, the graphic image will be brought to the current browser window.

<A HREF="picture.jpg">A nice picture!</A>

Anchors are also used to define named locations in a document as targets for hypertext links. For example if this anchor is placed immediately below the <BODY> tag of a page

<A NAME="top"></A>

and the link below is placed anywhere in the page

<A HREF="#top">Jump to top of page</A>

clicking the 'Jump to top of page' link will cause the browser to do just that.

NAME should be a string defining a unique name for the HTML document in which it is placed. Placing a file name and path before the # in a link tag lets you open a different page at a specific place.

Images:

Images, or pictures, have made a big difference in the way that Web pages look. Probably there would not have been the enormous expansion of interest in the Internet if inline images had not been added to the Web.

<IMG SRC="picture.jpg">

The above example shows the simplest way to add an inline image to a page. You can wrap it inside anchor tags and then it will be a 'clickable' image, as below:

<A HREF="largepic.jpg"><IMG SRC="pic.jpg"></A>

Here, when the image *pic.jpg* is clicked with the mouse the browser will display the other image *largepic.jpg*. To return to the original page the user would then have to use the browser's Back button.

The IMG element supports the following attributes:

SRC is required for every IMG element. It specifies a URL for the image resource, for instance a GIF, JPEG or PNG image file.

ALT is used to provide a text description of the image. This is vital so that speech-based and text only browsers can follow your pages.

ALIGN specifies how the image is positioned relative to the current line of text in which it occurs:

ALIGN=TOP   positions the top of the image with the top of the current text line.

ALIGN=MIDDLE   aligns the middle of the image with the baseline for the current line of text.

ALIGN=BOTTOM is the default and aligns the bottom of the image with the baseline.

ALIGN=LEFT   floats the image to the current left margin so that subsequent text is flowed along the image's right-hand side.

ALIGN=RIGHT   floats the image to the current right margin so that subsequent text is flowed along the image's left-hand side.

You can also use the <BR> tag attributes to control text flow round images as mentioned on page 64.

WIDTH specifies the intended width of the image in pixels. When given together with the height, this allows browsers to reserve screen space for the image before the image data has arrived over the network.

HEIGHT specifies the required height of the image in pixels.

BORDER sets the width of a border in pixels. Used when the IMG element is part of a link and, by default, browsers usually place a coloured border (typically blue) around the image. Use BORDER=0 to suppress the border altogether.

HSPACE can be used to provide white space to the immediate left and right of the image. The HSPACE attribute sets the width of this white space in pixels. By default HSPACE is a small non-zero number.

VSPACE is used to provide white space above and below the image in the same way.

Our example below shows the code for an image with all the above attributes being used as a link to another graphic file:

```
<A HREF="largecat.jpg">
    <IMG SRC="pcat.jpg"
        ALIGN=LEFT WIDTH=125 HEIGHT=72
        ALT="A Persian cat"
        BORDER=0 HSPACE=10 VSPACE=10>
</A>
```

Lists:

HTML supports several kinds of structured lists. The most important ones are:

1. Ordered.
2. Unordered.
3. Definition.

An **ordered** list, like that shown above, has its items numbered. The code to make this list is as follows:

```
<OL>
<LI>Ordered.</LI>
<LI>Unordered.</LI>
<LI>Definition.</LI>
</OL>
```

For an **unordered** list, with bullets and no numbering, you simply change one letter in the opening and closing tags:

```
<UL>
<LI>Ordered.</LI>
<LI>Unordered.</LI>
<LI>Definition.</LI>
</UL>
```

In these two types of list you can actually control the type of bullets used and the numbering system, but we do not have the space here to cover everything!

The other main type is a **definition** list which looks something like this:

Ordered Lists.
> The list items are numbered.

Unordered Lists.
> A simple list with bullets.

Definition Lists.
> Each item has a title and a description.

The code to make this list is as follows:

```
<DL>
<DT>Ordered Lists.</DT>
<DD>The list items are numbered.</DD>
<P>
<DT>Unordered Lists.</DT>
<DD>A simple list with bullets.</DD>
<P>
<DT>Definition Lists.</DT>
<DD>Each item has a title and a description.</DD>
</DL>
```

Lists can be nested to produce quite complicated results, but we will leave it to you to experiment with these. Take care though, if you nest too many levels you may have problems getting the code to work, due to complexity.

Horizontal Rules:

Horizontal lines across a page can often be usefully used in a Web page, but don't go overboard with them. They can break a page up too much and even spoil the layout.

The <HR> element places a line and no end tag is required. The line produced can be controlled by placing any of the following attributes inside the tag:

ALIGN determines whether the rule is placed at the left, centre or right of the space between the current margins. By default, the rule is centred.

NOSHADE renders the line in a solid colour rather than as the traditional two colour 'groove'.

SIZE can be used to set the height of the line in pixels.

WIDTH can be used to set the width of the rule (or the length of the line) in pixels (e.g. WIDTH=100) or as the percentage between the current left and right margins (e.g. WIDTH="50%"). The default is 100%, or full width.

<HR SIZE=4 WIDTH=50% NOSHADE>

As an example, the code above will produce a centred solid line 4 pixels thick and half the width of the page, as shown below:

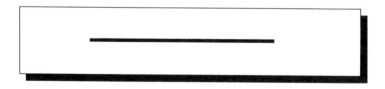

Character Formatting

HTML has two types of formatting styles for individual words or sentences: logical and physical. With logical styles you tag text according to its meaning, such as the **Emphasis** tag <EM>, while with the most often used physical styles you simply indicate the specific appearance of a section, such as **bold** <B> or **italics** <I>. They all require start and end tags to control the actual text to be formatted.

The logical styles are not used very much. They were originally designed when Web documents contained only 'academic' type text and virtually no graphics. These days control of actual presentation is getting more and more important and authors prefer to set text to italics when that is what they want, rather than use the <EM> tag, which may also italicise. With the introduction of style sheets in the latest browsers this trend may well reverse though.

Text level elements must be properly nested or some browsers will not render the effects correctly. The following line is correct,

This has some <B>bold and <I>italic text</I></B>

but the next one has crossed links and may not work.

This has some <B>bold and <I>italic text</B></I>

Logical Elements:

<EM>	basic emphasis which is typically displayed in an italic font.
<STRONG>	strong emphasis which is typically rendered in a bold font.
<CODE>	used for extracts from program code. Displayed in fixed-width font.

<DFN>	for defining a word, typically displayed in italics.
<SAMP>	used for sample output from programs, and scripts, etc., displayed in fixed width font.
<KBD>	used for text to be typed by the user, displayed in fixed-width font.
<VAR>	used for variables or arguments to commands, typically displayed in italics.
<CITE>	used for citations or references to other sources, typically displayed in italics.

Physical Elements:

<B>	bold text style
<I>	italic text style
<U>	underlined text style
<STRIKE>	strike-through text style
<SUB >	places text in subscript style
<SUP>	places text in superscript style
<TT>	teletype or monospaced text
<BIG>	places text in a large font
<SMALL>	places text in a small font

The example below shows the result of using some of these formatting styles.

Bold *Italic* <u>Underlined</u> ~~Strikethrough~~ Big Small Subscript Superscript
Strong *Citation* Code Sample *Emphasis* Fixed width *Variable* Key board

72

Preformatted Text:

Use the 'preformatted' tag <PRE> to generate text in a fixed-width font and displayed exactly as it is entered. Multiple spaces, new lines, other characters and tabs all display in the same locations as in the source HTML file. This is useful for program listings, and other things. For example, the following Visual BASIC code lines placed inside <PRE> tags:

```
<PRE>
Begin Menu mnuOptions
 Caption    = "&Options"
    Begin Menu mnuVATRate
       Caption    = "&VAT Rate"
    End
    Begin Menu mnuAbout
       Caption    = "&About"
    End
    Begin Menu mnuExit
       Caption    = "E&xit"
    End
 End
End
</PRE>
```

should display in your browser as:

```
Begin Menu mnuOptions
 Caption    = "&Options"
    Begin Menu mnuVATRate
       Caption    = "&VAT Rate"
    End
    Begin Menu mnuAbout
       Caption    = "&About"
    End
    Begin Menu mnuExit
       Caption    = "E&xit"
    End
 End
End
```

The <PRE> tag can be used with an optional WIDTH attribute that specifies the maximum number of characters for a line and signals your browser to choose an appropriate font and indentation for the text.

Hyperlinks can be used within <PRE> sections, but because the characters '<', '>' and '&' have special meanings in HTML, you must use their escape sequences, < - > - & - respectively, to enter them.

Blockquote:

You can use the <BLOCKQUOTE> tag to include lengthy quotations in a separate block of text on the screen. Browsers generally change the margins for the quotation to separate it from surrounding text.

The Address Tag:

The <ADDRESS> tag is usually used to 'stamp' the bottom of a Web page with details of the page author, an e-mail address, and the last revision date of the page. It is usually the last item in a file. It is good practice to give this information so that the reader can tell the source of the document and how old it is, which should help to evaluate its relevance.

As an example, the last few lines of our code generated in the last chapter should look similar to those below:

```
<CENTER>
<ADDRESS>Site maintained by
<A HREF="MAILTO:prmolive@csm.ex.ac.uk">Phil
Oliver</A>
.   Last modified on 28 July 1998
</ADDRESS>
</CENTER>
```

An Easy Way to Centre Anything:

The example on the previous page also shows the easiest way to force almost anything in HTML to be centre formatted. You can use the <CENTER> opening and </CENTER> closing tags to surround what you want centred.

This tag was introduced by Netscape but is retained in standard HTML (v3.2 and above) because of its widespread use. It may not always work as expected in Microsoft browsers though!

Some Font Control

The <FONT> element, which requires start and end tags, allows you to change the font face (type), size and colour of any text enclosed by its tags. Font sizes are not specific but are given in terms of a scalar range of 1 to 7, set by the browser, the default font size being 3 in most cases, which equates to a point size of 12. The problem for page designers is that the browser user can reset the font size his browser defaults to. This can ruin the formatting of any text based page. To help get over this you can use the BASEFONT element as described later.

The attributes accepted by the FONT element are:

SIZE   This sets the font size for the text
                concerned. Size can be an integer
                ranging from 1 to 7 for an absolute font
                size, or a relative font size with a signed
                integer value, e.g. SIZE="+2" or
                SIZE="-1". This is mapped to an
                absolute font size by adding it to a
                default size of 3, or to the current base
                font size set by the BASEFONT element
                (see page 77).

COLOR   Used to set the colour of the text.
         Colours are given as RGB in
         hexadecimal notation, or as one of 16
         widely understood colour names given
         earlier in the chapter (page 63).

FACE   Newer browsers support a FACE
         attribute which accepts a comma
         separated list of font names in order of
         preference. The browser works through
         the list and searches for an installed
         font with the corresponding name, or
         ignores the FACE command if it does
         not find any of them.

The example below shows the FONT element with all
its attributes used, along with the resulting text that
was displayed. You will have to take our word for it, but
the text was red.

```
<FONT
    FACE="Courier New"
    COLOR="#FF0000"
    SIZE=+2>
    This will produce red, large fixed-width text
</FONT>
```

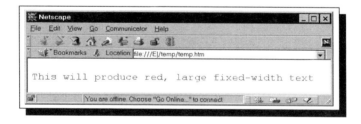

The BASEFONT Tag:

This single tag can be used once in a document. It is placed at the top of the <BODY> section and is used to set the base font details for a document. This is useful as it overrides any font settings the user may have set, so your page is more likely to format correctly.

The attributes of BASEFONT are the same as those for the FONT element, namely FACE, SIZE and COLOR, as shown in the example below.

```
<HTML>
<HEAD>
.....
<BASEFONT  FACE="Arial, Helvetica, Sans Serif"
COLOR= "black" SIZE=2>
</HEAD>
```

You should remember that the base font size applies to the normal and preformatted text on a page but not to headings, unless they have been modified using the FONT element with a relative font size.

Tables

In HTML, tables are used to display tabular material or more commonly for layout purposes, as we shall see in the next chapter. An example of a simple table containing text is shown below:

An Example of a Table		
Name	**Tag**	**Typical Appearance**
Table	**TABLE**	A table like this with border
Caption	**CAPTION**	A title as shown above
Row	**TR**	A row
Head	**TH**	Bold, centered heading
Data	**TD**	Plain, left aligned

The code for this table could look like that below, but with some browsers you may have to add end tags to the ROW, HEADER and DATA elements:

```
<TABLE BORDER=2 CELLPADDING=8 ALIGN=CENTER>
<CAPTION>An Example of a Table</CAPTION>
<TR><TH> Name <TH> Tag <TH> Typical Appearance
<TR><TH> Table <TH> TABLE <TD> A table like this with
border
<TR><TH> Caption <TH> CAPTION <TD> A title as shown
above
<TR><TH> Row <TH> TR <TD> A row
<TR><TH> Head <TH> TH <TD> Bold, centered heading
<TR><TH> Data <TH> TD <TD> Plain, left aligned
</TABLE>
```

The attributes in the <TABLE> tag listed below are all optional. By default, the table is drawn without a surrounding border and is sized automatically to fit the contents. A caption, or table title, is placed at the top or bottom of the table depending on the ALIGN attribute used.

Each table row is contained in a <TR> element, although the end tag can be omitted. Table cells are defined by <TD> tags for data and <TH> tags for headers. Like <TR>, these are containers but can be given without trailing end tags.

A table cell can contain a wide variety of other block and text level elements including graphics and even other tables. This is what makes tables so important in building Web pages. When their borders are switched off they are transparent, you can then place them anywhere on your page to act as layout holders for text, graphics, or any other elements.

Table Attributes:

The <TABLE> element always requires both start and end tags, and can have the following attributes:

ALIGN
This takes one of the values: LEFT, CENTER or RIGHT. It specifies the horizontal placement of the table relative to the current left and right margins. It defaults to left alignment. This is not supported by Netscape browsers prior to version 4.

WIDTH
The table width is automatically determined from the table contents, but you can use the WIDTH attribute to set the table width to a fixed value in pixels (e.g. WIDTH=325), or as a percentage of the space between the current left and right margins.

BORDER	This attribute can be used to specify the width of an outer border around the table in pixels (e.g. BORDER=2). Setting this to zero will suppress the border altogether, which is the default when this attribute is not used.
CELLSPACING	In HTML each cell is given its own border which is separated from the borders around neighbouring cells. This separation can be set in pixels using the CELLSPACING attribute, (e.g. CELLSPACING=8). The same value also determines the separation between the table border and the borders of the outermost cells.
CELLPADDING	This sets the padding in pixels between the border around each cell and the cell's contents.

Table Captions:

The CAPTION element has one attribute ALIGN, which can be either ALIGN=TOP or ALIGN=BOTTOM. This can be used to force the caption to be placed above the top or below the bottom of the table, respectively. Most browsers default to placing the caption above the table. CAPTION always requires both start and end tags and the caption is limited to plain text and text-level formatting elements.

Table Rows:

The <TR> or table row element requires a start tag, but the end tag can be left out. <TR> acts as a container for table cells and has two attributes:

ALIGN   Sets the horizontal alignment of cell
             contents. It takes one of the case
             insensitive values: LEFT, CENTER or
             RIGHT and plays the same role as the
             ALIGN attribute on paragraph elements.

VALIGN   This can be used to set the default
             vertical alignment of cell contents within
             each cell. It takes one of the case
             insensitive values: TOP, MIDDLE or
             BOTTOM to position the cell contents.

Header and Data Cells:

There are two elements for defining table cells. <TH>
is used for header cells and <TD> for data cells. This
distinction allows browsers to render header and data
cells in different fonts, and enables speech based
browsers to do a better job. The start tags for <TH>
and <TD> are always needed but the end tags can be
left out. Table cells can have the following attributes:

NOWRAP   This attribute disables automatic
             word wrap within the contents of a
             cell.

ROWSPAN   Specifies the number of rows
             spanned by a cell, defaults to
             one.

COLSPAN   Specifies the number of columns
             spanned by a cell, the default is
             one.

ALIGN   Specifies the default horizontal
             alignment of cell contents, and
             overrides the ALIGN attribute on
             the table row. It takes the same
             values: LEFT, CENTER and
             RIGHT. If none is set for the cell,
             the default is left alignment for
             <TD> and CENTER alignment for

<TH>, but an ALIGN attribute in the <TR> element will then override this.

VALIGN   Specifies the default vertical alignment of cell contents, overriding the VALIGN attribute on the table row. It takes the same values of TOP, MIDDLE and BOTTOM. If none is set in the cell the default is middle, but a VALIGN attribute in the <TR> element will then override this.

WIDTH   Specifies the suggested width for a cell content in pixels or %. This value will normally be used unless it conflicts with the width requirements for other cells in the same column.

HEIGHT   Specifies the suggested height for a cell content in pixels. Again this value will normally be used unless it conflicts with the height requirements for other cells in the same row.

That is all the HTML we are going to cover here. It is enough to get you going and to let you build the type of Web sites we cover in this book.

The language obviously contains very much more. Features such as Frames, that allow you to open multiple Web pages in the same window; Forms that allow a user to send you information from your Web page and Style Sheets for standardising formatting throughout a site can all come in very useful.

Then of course if you really want to get carried away there are several Scripting languages, like Javascript, you could learn to add other features to your sites. The scope is almost unlimited!

More Information on HTML

If you are on-line it is very easy to get all the information you want on HTML. Our favourite site for this has the highly original name of **Sizzling HTML Jalfrezi**. This gives a full on-line reference manual for HTML, complete with examples of all the code in use. Very well worth a visit, whether you are an absolute beginner, or an experienced page author. The URL is:

http://vzone.virgin.net/sizzling.jalfrezi

The site is free, but to get even more use from it you can send the author a cheque 'to cover the cost of a couple of beers' and he will send you the whole site on disc, or by e-mail, for you to load on your hard disc. We have found this very useful.

Another site with a good HTML tutorial is called **So, you want to make a Web Page**. When we last tried, entering the URL

http://junior.apk.net/~jbarta/webtutor.exe

would automatically download a self-extracting file containing all the tutorials.

Double-clicking this file will install them on the hard disc of your computer, so that you can look at them in your own time.

7. USING AN HTML EDITOR

If you have worked through the last two chapters you should be fairly happy using a WYSIWYG editor, like Composer, to visually prepare the basis of a Web page. You should also understand much of the HTML code that such an editor creates. We find that most WYSIWYG editors 'almost' produce the visual effects we want, but not quite. To finish a page you almost always have to fine tune the code manually.

This is where HTML editors come in. There are many different ones available, but most of them provide a menu system and icons that you activate to create the required HTML tags for your page. To use them you have to know what tags you need, but you do not have to remember all the details or spelling. Ideal if your memory is as bad as ours!

HTML Notepad

The editor we use most is HTML Notepad and the rest of this chapter will be based around this program. It is English shareware, and is published by Cranial Software who have a Web site at:

http://www.cranial.demon.co.uk

If you have not done so already, you can quickly download it from there. We will also include it as shareware on the Companion Disc, mentioned on the last page of this book.

HTML Notepad was originally designed as an assistant for the construction of HTML pages rather than the only tool you should use. It was intended for editing documents after they had been constructed by a WYSIWYG type editor. Since then it has grown to include most of the tools required, and we have in fact now completely given up using other editors and construct all our own pages with HTML Notepad.

Installing HTML Notepad:

The method of installing the program will depend on how you obtained it.

If you downloaded it from Cranial Software's Web site you must first unzip the downloaded file *htmln295.zip* in the folder where you want to keep it, and then continue from 2 below.

For a Companion Disc version:

1 Copy the files and folders from the HTML Notepad folder on the disc to a folder on your hard disc.

2 From Windows 95/98, right-click on the Task bar, select the **P**roperties option and then the **Start Menu Programs** tab control. Next click **A**dd and use the Program Wizard. First **B**rowse for the executable file *htmlnote.exe* in whatever folder you put it, then place the shortcut in the menu folder of your choice and select a name.

You could also drag the *htmlnote.exe* file icon, with the right mouse button depressed, from its folder to the desktop and opt to **Create** **S**hortcut when you release the button. If you release it over the Start button itself, it will add the program to the Start menu.

The Program Window:

When you first open HTML Notepad (by clicking one of the menu options or shortcuts created above) it displays a simple window as shown on the next page. This has a menu system and a row of buttons, or icons and an editing area. If you widen the window, by dragging its right border to the right, the menu will eventually click up and take one line only.

When you move the pointer over a button a message flag indicates the function of that button. Most of these will be described in the next few pages.

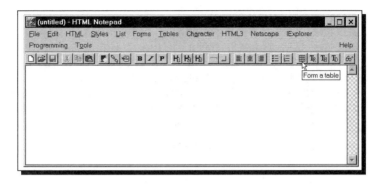

Before getting too involved there are two things you should do to 'set up' your program.

Setting up for your Browser:

The Test Page button, shown here, opens your Web browser and loads the page you are working on. This lets you see the results of your work from time to time. For this to work, the program needs to know which browsers you have on your system. Select the **Tools**, **Browsers Setup** menu option and then the **Add** button. You then search for the executable file of your browser and add it to the list of setup browsers. Lastly, select the browser you wish to use most from the list and click the **Set Default** button and press **OK** to complete the process. The Test Page button will then let you test a saved page.

Setting your New Page Template:

The **File**, **New** menu option, or the New toolbar button shown here, will open a dialogue box listing the files in the template folder. Initially there are probably three, but you should edit these default templates and add your own as time goes by. A template file contains the HTML code that you want placed in every new page you create. It saves a lot of time.

Select *initial.htm(l)* which opens an (untitled) file with the initial default HTML settings provided by Cranial. After the last chapter most of these will have some meaning to you, but there is no real need to understand them yet. We suggest that now, before you go any further, you amend the contents of this page to those below, but put your own details in the three underlined sections of course!

```
<HTML>
<HEAD>
<TITLE></TITLE>
<META NAME="Author" CONTENT="Phil Oliver">
<META NAME="Description" CONTENT="">
<META NAME="KeyWords" CONTENT="">
</HEAD>

<BODY TEXT="#000000" BGCOLOR="#FFFFFF"
LINK="#0000EE" VLINK="#551A8B" ALINK="#FF0000">


<HR SIZE=3 WIDTH="250">
<CENTER>
<ADDRESS>
This page is maintained by <A
HREF="mailto:prmolive@csm.ex.ac.uk">Phil Oliver
</A><BR>
Last updated on ...
</ADDRESS>
</CENTER>

</BODY>
</HTML>
```

If you don't want to type it, there is a file on the disc, or at the Web site, called *template.htm* to help out.

When you have the text you want in this page, use the **File**, **Save As** command and open the Template folder which should be located in the folder where HTML Notepad is stored. Save the file back as *initial.html* overwriting the original one. That's it.

Building a Site Page

When you click the New button from now on, and select the *initial.html* template, the new page that opens will show all your code and text. Don't worry, when you try to save it next, you will be asked to rename it, so as not to spoil the template.

We will now step through the process of building the next page of our Web site, *artist.htm*, as shown below.

Michael Strang, St Ives - Tate Gallery in background

Michael Strang has a Diploma in Art and Design (Hons) London, and studied at the Wimbledon and Camberwell Schools of Art.

He lives in Cornwall and paints landscapes, still lifes, portraits and other subjects, mainly in oils, but sometimes water colour. **He accepts commissions**, and his work can be found in various collections in Canada, the USA, Switzerland, Germany, Corsica and the United Kingdom.

A painting is but a prayer;
a communion with the very essence of life.
And sometimes an answer rises from unfathomable depths,
a voice of silence woven into the pigments.

He has been painting since 1973, supports many charitable causes and has shown in an impressive list of galleries, including:

Royal Academy - London	Tate Gallery - St Ives*	Mall Gallery - London
New Craftsman - St Ives	CSM Gallery	George Frederick Watts Gallery
Member Chelsea Arts Club	Cornwall Education Collection	Bryan Forbes Gallery

* A series of over 50 small Porthmeor Paintings were shown at the Tate Gallery, St Ives in their "Century of Images" exhibition from April to October 1995.

Home | Gallery | Main Site

This page is maintained by Phil Oliver
Last updated 28 July 1998

As you can see, this page gives some background details of the artist and has a couple of graphics to make it a little more interesting.

Inserting Tables:

We will use two tables in this page, the first to limit the overall width of the page data to 600 pixels, which should then fit onto most users' screens, and the second to display the tabular text at the bottom of the page. The first one will form a container for all the body data, including the other table which will be nested in it.

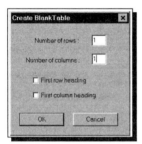

Place the insertion point under the <BODY..> tag of the new file and action the **Tables**, **Create Blank Table** command. This will open the dialogue box shown here. Set the **Number of rows** and the **Number of columns** both to 1 and press the **OK** button.

The editor will automatically add the basic code tags for a table with one row and one column, as shown below (after we have placed a few hard returns between the opening and closing <TD> tags).

```
<TABLE BORDER=1>
<TR><TD>

</TD></TR>
</TABLE>
```

We do not want a border for this table, so change the BORDER attribute to 0 and type WIDTH=600 followed by a space between the 0 and the tag's closing > bracket. Then immediately click the Center

alignment button shown here. This will add the last attribute needed inside this tag as shown overleaf.

<TABLE BORDER=0 WIDTH=600 ALIGN="CENTER">

The ALIGN="CENTER" attribute will centre the table with most browsers, but not all, so we will include the whole table code in <CENTER> tags as well. To do this select the whole table (within the <TABLE> tags) and select **Center** from the **Netscape** menu.

This finishes the outer container table, all its contents will now be placed within the <TD> </TD> tags. You may by now have worked out that to place tag elements you can select the data first and they are placed round that data when you action the command. To place attributes you place the cursor in the required tag and action the command. You can also, if you prefer, place element tags at the insertion point and then type the data between them.

You should have no problem now adding the other table which is nested inside the first table's <TD> </TD> tags. We suggest you leave a few strategic blank lines in the code so as not to get confused.

```
<CENTER>
<TABLE BORDER=1  CELLPADDING=3
ALIGN="CENTER">
<TR>
   <TD>Royal Academy - London</TD>
   <TD>Tate Gallery - St Ives*</TD>
   <TD>Mall Gallery - London</TD>
</TR>
<TR>
   <TD>New Craftsman - St Ives </TD>
   <TD>CSM Gallery</TD>
   <TD>George Frederick Watts Gallery</TD>
</TR>
<TR>
   <TD>Member Chelsea Arts Club </TD>
   <TD>Cornwall Education Collection </TD>
   <TD>Bryan Forbes Gallery</TD>
</TR>
</TABLE>
</CENTER>
```

Adding a Graphic:

We actually added the second table out of sequence to show how tables can fit inside each other. We must now go to the top of the page and add the pictures and text that are above the inner table. Place the insertion point above the opening <CENTER> tag of the inside table code you entered, and click the Insert Image button shown here on the left. The Select Image Source dialogue box is opened for you to complete.

Complete this box, as shown above, but for this to actually work you need to have obtained the image files as outlined on page 36 in an earlier chapter. You should also be working in the same folder that they are stored in. When you press **OK** the following code will be placed for you:

<IMG SRC="tate.jpg" WIDTH=260 HEIGHT=171 ALT="The artist in front of St Ives Tate gallery">

The image dimensions above are actually less than those of the full size image, so to let anyone view the full size photograph we will create a link so that when the thumbnail is clicked it will be displayed.

 This is very easy to do. Highlight all of the <IMG...> tag shown above and click the Anchor HREF button. Type the file name *tate.jpg* into the Select Reference Link box and press **OK**. This places the <A HREF> tag element around the <IMG...> tag.

<A HREF="tate.jpg"> ... </A>

Before we go any further add the BORDER=0 attribute to the image attributes, otherwise an ugly blue or purple border will be placed round the photograph to show that it is a link.

We want a caption under the photo-graph, so force a new line after the closing </A> tag by clicking the Line Break button, shown here.

Next type the following text,

Michael Strang, St Ives - Tate Gallery in background

highlight it and click the Bold button which places <B> </B> tags round the text. Without removing the selection, open the **Netscape** menu, select **Font Size** and type -2 in the **Size** box as shown here on the right. This

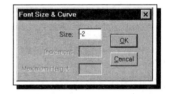

places the code tags below around the text, to reduce its size by 2 factors.

<FONT SIZE=-2><B>Michael ...</B></FONT>

Lastly, place <CENTER> tags round the whole of this section of code.

If you have not done so already, save the file by clicking the Save button and give it the name *artist.htm*.

When you open the file into your browser it should be starting to look like ours shown a few pages back. If some sections do not appear at all in your browser, you may have some of the table tags mixed up, or omitted. In this case it may help to study the whole page code given in Appendix A.

Adding a Background Image:

So far, the code we have placed will render the background of the page in plain white. This can be a little wearing on the eyes, so we will add the same background image that was used in the Home page earlier on. Using the same background over a whole site helps to give it an identity.

To do this just position the insertion point inside the end > bracket of the <BODY..> tag and type

BACKGROUND="background.gif"

As we saw in the last chapter, the other attributes in the <BODY> tag control the colours of the text, links and background that will display when the page is opened. The attribute BGCOLOR="#FFFFFF" sets the background colour to white. You should still use this even when you use a background image. This is the colour that displays until the image loads and with a slow transmission this can take several seconds.

Adding Text Paragraphs:

When you enter text into HTML you have to place tags to help browsers split it into paragraphs, or sections. Otherwise the text will just render as one continuous 'mass'.

The usual way to do this is with the <P> paragraph tag, which is placed by clicking the Paragraph button. In our example we have added the attribute ALIGN="JUSTIFY" to all the text paragraph tags. On newer browsers this aligns the text flush with both the left and right margins, the same as the text in this book. With older browsers this will just be ignored.

<P ALIGN="JUSTIFY">......</P>

Unfortunately, at the time of writing, HTML Notepad does not support this attribute and you will have to add it manually. The easiest way is to type it once and then copy and paste it everywhere else.

If you want to enter all the text for the example it is given in the example code in Appendix A. You can either place the <P> tags and then type the text between them, or type the text first, highlight it, and then click the Paragraph button to place the tags.

Placing the second image should be easier than the first as it is not used as a link. As before, click the Insert Image button and complete the Select Image Source dialogue box with the following details.

Image source   text.jpg
Width   414
Height   108
Alternative text   A painting is but a prayer

Special Characters:

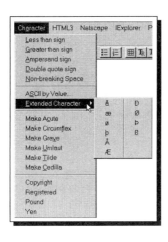

In the last paragraph of text inverted commas are used to surround a title. In HTML this character, as well as several others, is often used as part of the code and requires special treatment.

Opening the **Character** menu and selecting **Double quote sign** will place the special character code

"

into your document. This must be placed whenever you want a " character to appear, and must be entered exactly as shown.

HTML Notepad lets you easily add these special characters as shown above. Others can be entered by looking their ASCII code up in Appendix B and using it in the **ASCII by value** menu option above.

95

The Menu Bar:

The easiest way to put a bar of menu options on a Web page is to use text 'options', linked to their destination files, and separated by vertical lines. In our example, as shown below, this menu line is also placed between two centred horizontal lines.

 The horizontal lines are easy to add. Using the Horizontal Rule button, shown here, just places the <HR> tag. In our case we want to add some attributes to control the line produced, so we could use the **HTML**, **HR Special** menu command, or <Ctrl+Alt+Enter> key combination, to open the Box shown here. Entering 3 in the **Size** field and 250 in the **Width** field and pressing **Ok** will place the code for the line as shown below.

<HR SIZE=3 WIDTH=250%>

Unfortunately the width attribute is taken as a %, fine if that is what you want, but we don't. We want the line set to 250 pixels wide, not varying depending on how wide the user's browser window is. It is easy, though, to amend the attribute to WIDTH="250".

The menu line code is shown complete at the top of the next page. To create this, first type the text itself:

Home I Gallery I Main Site

Highlight 'Home', click the Anchor HREF button and type *index.htm* as the link reference. Repeat this for the other two options, but giving gallery.htm and http://www.michaelstrang.com as the link references in turn. Highlight the whole section of code and set the Font Size to +1 and then add <CENTER> tags as before. With a little editing for the sake of clarity the menu section should look like ours below.

```
<CENTER><FONT SIZE=+1>
  <A HREF="index.htm">Home</A> I
  <A HREF="gallery.htm">Gallery</A> I
  <A HREF="http://www.michaelstrang.com">Main
  Site</A>
</FONT></CENTER>
```

Another way to build a menu bar is to use a series of button images with the menu text written on them, as we show below. To do this you need to be able to use a graphics program like PaintShopPro for example. Make sure you put alternative text behind the images.

Using Comments:

If you look at our example code in Appendix A you will see that we have added 'Comments' to make the text a little easier to both understand and follow. This is always a good idea, but we must own up to the fact that we don't often do it.

To place a comment in your code where your insertion point is located, just use the **HTML**, **Comment** command and type the comment text between the tags created, as follows.

```
<!---This is a comment --->
```

Like white space, all browsers ignore any text that is 'commented out'. Try and get into the habit of doing this.

The Page HEAD Section:

As we saw in an earlier chapter the information in the HEAD section of a Web page does not show on the screen, but is very important to its general success. The template we have created has slots for you to at least enter the following document details:

Title
Description
KeyWords

Title - This gives the text you want to appear in the window title bar when the document is browsed. This is how many Web search tools locate specific Web pages, so if you want readers to be able to locate your page easily, select a useful title that conveys what your page is all about. Keep the title short though, because this is also the text that browsers include when you bookmark a Web page.

Description - A few words describing the contents of the page. This is usually the information that readers are given about the page when a search tool, or engine, locates it in a search for a specific topic.

Keywords - Enter here the words and combinations of words relevant to your page that you think people may use when searching for a site like yours.

What you place in these boxes is critical to how successful your Web site will be. As we have already mentioned, there are millions of Web pages available for users to find, so you have to help the search engines both to locate your site and then to present it so that people will want to choose it from a long list of alternative choices.

You can see what we have placed in our examples in Appendix A to give you an idea. The more time and care you spend here, the more people you should eventually get to successfully search for your site, and of course, to visit it.

The Last Site Page

There is one more page to create in our example Web site. This is called *gallery.htm* and consists of a small range of paintings with some background detail of each, as shown below.

We shall not spend long here on this page, as by now you should be able to build most of this on your own. The whole code is included in Appendix A.

If you use the previous file *artist.htm* as a template you can delete the text and graphics not required and modify the menu to give yourself a flying start.

Image Alignment:

We think the success of this page depends on the accurate alignment of the thumbnail pictures and their accompanying text, and have used this technique on several gallery type pages on our Art sites.

Firstly all the thumbnail images are created the same size, in this case 112 pixels wide by 80 high. This not only helps the layout, but with file sizes of only 2 or 3KB, means they load onto the page very rapidly.

The ALIGN=LEFT attribute in the <IMG..> tag forces the image to the left margin and allows text to wrap to the right around it. As you might expect, you place this by clicking the Insert Left Alignment button shown here.

To create a suitable left margin for the wrapped text and to keep it away from the image, you use the HSPACE attribute, to create 'horizontal space'. In our case HSPACE=40. This is placed in HTML Notepad with the **Netscape**, **Image HSpace** command. If you had a lot of text wrapping round the image you would need to use the VSPACE attribute to give it vertical space as well.

In our gallery example we want the image caption text to be placed alongside its respective thumbnail, and any space below to be left blank. This is done with the Line Break tag <BR>, but with the attribute CLEAR="ALL" added to it. You add this in two parts, first click the Line Break button, then with the insertion point in the tag but behind the BR, use the **HTML**, **Clear**, **All** menu command.

We could have used the CLEAR="LEFT" attribute, which clears text that flows only around a left-aligned image. CLEAR="ALL" clears text until it can reach both full margins.

We will leave it to you to complete the gallery page now. Have fun.

Some Site Improvements

Well, that completes the construction of our small sample Web site. If you have followed our ideas we hope you enjoyed them. By now you should be well capable of adapting them to a site of your own.

There are many ways we could improve our site. We could have used tables much more extensively to control page widths and the location of our data. In the gallery, for example, we could have placed each image and its caption in two data cells of a table row. By adjusting the cell dimensions and alignment we could have achieved many different layouts. When you remember that people use many different browsers on computers with their screens set to one of several resolutions, this may have been a good idea to try and achieve a standard page 'view'.

A major weakness of our site is that when the full size images are opened they open into a full browser window with the picture in the top left hand corner. The background colour will also depend on the particular browser settings.

This could easily be controlled by giving each full size image its own HTML page. You could then set the background of this page and image orientation however you want. You would, of course, have to link to the page from the thumbnail, not to the image itself. You would also need some links on the page to return to the main site.

We will leave it to you to think of any more improvements. They are limitless. That is the one thing about Web page building, the more you do, the better you get. Hopefully.

....

This chapter should have introduced you to the editor HTML Notepad, but we suggest that you work your way through all the other buttons and menu commands on your own to see which tags they produce.

Don't forget the Help system, it is quite good and includes an overview of HTML itself.

....

8. GOING LIVE AT LAST

Well, so far we have built a small Web site and in the process taught ourselves a little about HTML. But, at the moment, our pages exist only on our local hard disc; we can browse them ourselves, but no one else can. The next step is to publish our site to a Web server. When you publish, you copy your Web pages (HTML and other files) to a Web server so that anyone on the Web can see what you've done.

A Web server, as we saw in an earlier chapter, is a program that runs all the time on a host computer and waits for Web clients' browsers to connect to it and request the files that make up a Web page. Servers and browsers communicate using the HyperText Transfer Protocol (HTTP), a language created for transferring hypertext documents over the Web.

Testing your Web Pages

One more thing to do, though, before we show the world our site. This is a very obvious step, but one that is sometimes not done very well. That is to test the pages to make sure the site has no mistakes, both in visual content, or in the HTML code.

Checking the Spelling:

Spelling mistakes on a Web site not only look bad, but they demonstrate that the page author could not be bothered to get the page checked. If you are a good speller, there should be no problem, just proof reading your work should be enough. If not, you could try and get someone else to look your new pages over. They might well have other useful comments to make about your efforts.

Another solution is to use a spell checker program. The latest version of Netscape's browser has one, which seems to work very well. It is a good idea to open each new page in turn in Netscape Composer, with the **File**, **Open Page** command, or the Open toolbar icon and then use the **Tools**, **Check Spelling** menu command, or the Check Spelling icon, shown above.

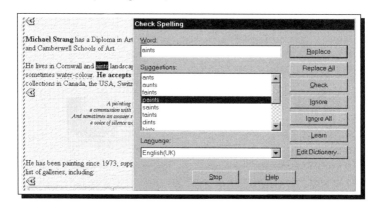

This scans the opened page, puts dotted red lines under suspect words, and opens the dialogue box shown above. The first time you use the Checker it will be set for the American English dictionary, so re-set the **Language** to English(UK), unless of course you are in the US! In our example above, the word 'aints' was not recognised (just as well) and the program gave a list of **Suggestions** as alternatives. We highlighted 'paints' and clicked **Replace** to cure the problem. Unusually 'water-colour' was also highlighted as being incorrect, and one of the two alternative options offered was, you've guessed it, 'water-colour'!

If no suitable suggestion is made, you can type a correction in the **Word** field, and then click **Replace** to substitute it for the mis-spelling, or **Replace All** to replace all occurrences in the document. Clicking **Ignore** leaves the selected word, whereas **Ignore All** leaves all occurrences of the selected word in the document.

Clicking **Check** verifies the entry in the **Word** field using the dictionary and **Learn** adds the entry to the dictionary and also replaces the selected word. Clicking **Edit Dictionary** displays a dialogue box you can use to add, replace, or remove words to and from the dictionary.

To stop checking the spelling at any time you click **Stop** and to close the dialogue box when the check is completed click the **Done** button. A lot of words to describe some fairly simple actions.

Checking Links:

Another thing you should check before you publish is that all the links on your site pages actually work.

Relative Links - Usually, when linking together your own pages, you use relative path names. In other words you describe other file locations **relative** to the page in question, as shown below.

link.htm	located in the current folder.
files/link.htm	located in the sub-folder called files, which is itself located in the current folder
..link.htm	located in the folder above the current folder. You can use multiple "../" to indicate a file location further up the directory structure.

Absolute Links - The alternative is to use the full path address, or URL, of the linked file, which is called an absolute link. If you use absolute links and then move your files, or rename a folder, then your links to these files may no longer work. You cannot check any absolute links to other sites unless you are on-line.

Checking links simply means working through each page and clicking each link in turn to make sure it sends you to the correct destination location or file. Not an exciting task, but essential if you want people to take your site seriously.

Checking File Names:

Web servers may be located on different platforms. For example, you may build your site on a Mac, or a PC running under Windows 98, but your server may operate under UNIX. Remember that filenames have different conventions and restrictions depending on the platform. So if you want your documents to be as portable between platforms as possible you should be very careful how you name the files of your site.

We find it safe to always follow the DOS 8.3 convention. File names being only 8 characters long with 3-character extensions and no spaces, upper case letters or other non-alphanumeric characters.

When we built our first site, we used Windows 95 long (and sensible) names for all our pages, such as *The Artist.htm*. All the links worked perfectly on our hard disc, but as soon as the files were on the server none of them were recognised at all.

Check all your file names and make sure none of them have any spaces or capital letters. This is easiest done in a File Management window, like My Computer in Windows 95 or 98. But if you do make any changes here don't forget to go back and re-check your links.

Sending to your Server

We discussed getting Web server space in an earlier chapter. Ideally, you'll be able to publish your Web pages using server space provided by the same organisation that gives you access to the Internet. These days all commercial Internet Service Providers (ISPs for short) have to offer Web space to stay competitive. Ask your system administrator if they offer Web server access and get full details of how to access it.

Once that is sorted out you must choose which way to connect and send your files. We offer two methods:

Using Netscape Composer:

The one-button publishing feature in Composer can make publishing your Web pages quick and easy, but not all servers will allow you to use this method. If you find that yours is one that does, try it out, but if not go straight to the next method.

To download all of our site in one operation you could follow the following procedure. First open the home page *index.htm* in the browser window, and then open it in a Composer window using one of the following methods.
Either use the **File**,
Edit Page menu command, or drag the **Location:** icon to the bottom right corner of the window and drop it onto the Composer icon, as shown in the two screen dumps here.

 Either method opens the file in a new Composer window. Now click the Publish icon, shown here, or use the **File**, **Publish** menu command to open the Publish dialogue box shown on the next page.

In our case the **Page Title** and **HTML Filename** fields are already completed, and if you select the **All files in page's folder** option a full list of the files in your working folder will be displayed in the **Other files to include** section. Clicking **Select All** will quickly select all the files you want to publish along with *index.htm*, in other words the whole site. One thing to remember here is that if a file on the remote server (where you're publishing) has the same filename as one that you are uploading, it will be replaced with the new one **without asking for confirmation**.

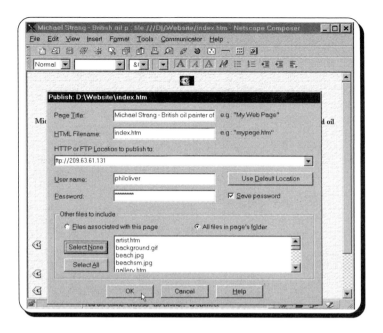

You may need to contact your Internet Service Provider to find out what to type in the next three fields. In the **HTTP or FTP Location to publish to** field you enter the location of the remote site you want to publish your Web pages to. The address we show is not real, so please do not use it. Once you've typed some locations here, in the future you can simply select from the drop-down list.

In the **User name** field you enter the name you type to access your Web pages on the server, and in the **Password** field, you enter the password to access the server. You should get both of these from your Internet Service Provider. The **Save Password** option saves this information so that you only need to type it the first time you use the procedure.

If you have previously specified settings in the Publish panel of the Composer Preferences dialogue box, you can click the **Use Default Location** to use these settings.

When the Publish box is completed, clicking the **OK** button may produce a warning box as shown here.

This just asks you to check that the links used on the page are correct. In our case we used mostly relative links and are happy with them, so just press **OK** to continue. The program is only checking for basic addressing mistakes before sending. This may also be followed by a security alert, which in our case, you can happily ignore.

Hopefully, if all is well and you are connected to the Internet, your files will be copied and your new site will be established on your server. You should be able to access them with your browser and see what everyone else has access to.

Using FTP:

We prefer to do all our file transfer work by FTP (File Transfer Protocol) itself. This gives you much more control and with the right program is no more difficult than copying files around your hard disc.

There are many FTP programs you can use. You may even have one on your PC. Our favourite is a small program called CuteFTP (see page 20). This is shareware, and you can download a version from

http://cuteftp.com/

and use it for four weeks, before you are asked to open your wallet for £20, or so. Well worth it, we think!

CuteFTP

CuteFTP Help

Release Notes

Uninstall CuteFTP

A quicker way to download a version of CuteFTP is from the TUCOWS mirror site at Lancaster University described on page 18. For Windows 95, 98 and NT the downloaded file is currently *cute2532.exe*. To install the program simply double click this file once it is saved to your hard disc. When you have followed the procedure offered, you will find four new icons in the menu folder you chose, as shown here.

The top one runs the actual program, the next, the Help file, is shown below. Have a look at the release notes if you want, but please don't use the last icon yet!

The Help for this program is superb. In fact it is so good we are going to insist you read their Chapter 3 before you go any further. We will not duplicate it here!

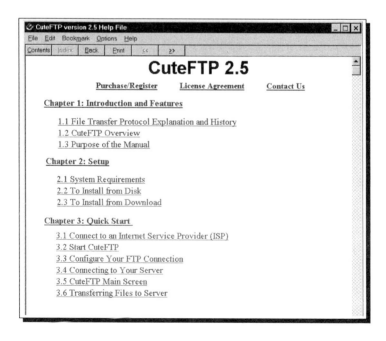

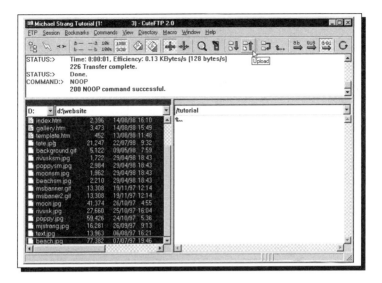

Our examples here show the uploading operation on the previous version of CuteFTP. The connection details on the title bars have been partially obscured for obvious reasons. With such a good Help system you don't need us to describe this in any detail.

Once the program is setup, configured and running, as described in their Help section, you simply highlight your folder and site in the Site Manager and click the **Connect** button. One thing though, is to make sure you are are actually on-line before you do this, otherwise the connection cannot be made.

The main screen, as shown above and on the next page, is used to move your files to the server. This is very much like the operation of other Windows' File Managers, but with the left window showing folders and files on your own disc, and the right one showing the folders and files of your distant server area. You select in the left window the files you want to move, drag them to the right window with your left mouse button depressed and release the button to drop them there. This starts the actual uploading operation. It's as simple as that, once you have the program configured.

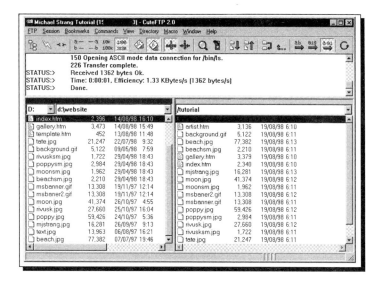

Making Sure it All Works

Once your site is on the server you will obviously want to check it out straight away, to make sure everything works as planned. Hopefully all will be well, and you won't have any bad links or missing files. Be rigorous with this check though, it is even more important than the one described earlier.

9. PROMOTING YOUR WEB SITE

The formula for success on the Internet begins with hard work. It takes perseverance, dedication and patience to get long term success. Those people who complain about wasting their money getting on the Internet are usually from the companies that just put their brochure on the Web, and expect the orders to flow in. It does not work that way. No matter how good the site is, people have to find it out of the millions that are there. This means a promotion policy is essential.

There are three main ways that Internet users locate the sites they visit. These entail using the search tools to look for sites with a certain content; following a link on another site, or entering a specific site address (URL) that they have seen and remembered somewhere else. Promoting your Web site involves all of these. You have to make sure the search tools know about your site and have the information to describe it properly. You also have to advertise it, and its address, as far and wide as you possibly can.

Web Searching Tools

There are two main types of search tools widely used on the Internet, search engines and directories. They are not the same, the difference being in how their listings are compiled.

Search engines, such as Excite and Alt Vista, create their listings automatically by 'crawling' the Web, then people search through what they have found.

Directories, such as Yahoo, depend on people like you for their listings. You submit a short description to the directory with the URL for your new site, which is then reviewed by one of their editors. A search request to the directory then looks for matches only in the descriptions submitted. Changing your web pages later on has no effect on your listing.

113

How Search Engines Work:

Search engines have three major elements. First is the spider, also called the robot, or crawler. This visits a web page, reads it, and then follows all, or some of, the links to other pages within the site. The spider returns to the site on a regular basis, maybe monthly, to look for changes.

Everything the spider finds goes into the second part of a search engine, the index. This is like a giant file containing a copy of the text of every web page that the spider finds. When you make changes to a web page and it is spidered again, then the index is updated.

Search engine software is the third part of a search engine. This is the program that sifts through the millions of pages recorded in the index to find matches to a search and rank them in order of what it believes is most relevant.

All search engines have these basic parts but they are set up in different ways, so the same search on different search engines will produce different results. We include a listing of the main search tools and some of their properties a little later on.

Search Ranking Methods:

When you use a search engine you enter the words, or a phrase, that you are interested in and press a button. Very quickly, usually, the search tool will sort through the millions of pages in its index and present you with a list of the ones it thinks match your topic. These will be ranked, so that the ones considered most relevant come first. As long as your site contains the searched-for keywords it will be listed, but where on the list?

Search engines all rank a Web page depending on the location and frequency of keywords on the page. Some then consider other criteria as well.

When the keywords appear in the page title they are considered more relevant and given a higher weighting. Next, if they appear near the top of a page, such as in the heading or in the first few paragraphs of text they also carry more weight.

Frequency is the other major factor in how search engines determine relevancy. The higher the ratio of keywords to other text on the page the higher will be the ranking. But you have to be very careful here. It is a common practice among more unscrupulous Web authors to load a page with hundreds of keywords that are not part of the actual text, purely to force higher search rankings. This practice is known as spamming and is heavily frowned on by the search engine providers. They penalise pages, or exclude them from the index completely, if they detect search engine spamming. So be warned.

Some search tools, like WebCrawler for example, use link popularity as part of their ranking method. Pages with more links pointing at them from other sites are given a slight boost to their ranking.

The use of keywords in meta tags can help with a page's ranking, especially with HotBot and Infoseek. If all else is equal then ranking is done alphabetically.

The Main Search Tools

In the next few pages we present a listing of the major search engines and directories that could be considered critical to the success of a Web site. You should try very hard to get your site registered with these as between them they probably control more than 95% of the searches carried out on the Web at the present time.

Like the rest of the Web though, this situation is very fluid. New search engines are being spawned all the time and existing ones are bought and sold.

AltaVista:

http://altavista.digital.com/

Opened in December 1995, AltaVista is run by Compaq and has gained widespread name recognition. It is consistently the largest search engine on the web, in terms of pages indexed, and is a particular favourite among researchers. It has a partnership with LookSmart that provides it with directory listings.

Linked at the bottom of a Yahoo search page, so is likely to be used if Yahoo (the most popular search tool) fails to find a match.

Main features that affect Web page design
(as of August 1998)

Total Web Pages in index	140 million
Pages crawled per day	10 million
Time for submitted pages to be indexed	1 day
Time for unsubmitted pages	1 to 30 days
Frames support	Yes
Image map support	Yes
Ranks link popularity	No
Ranks meta tags	No
Indexes image Alt text	Yes
Indexes comments	No
Case sensitive	Yes
Maximum title length	78 characters
Maximum description length	150 characters
Meta tag display support	Yes
Shows last modified date	Yes

Excite:

http://www.excite.com/

Launched in late 1995, Excite grew quickly in prominence and rapidly consumed two of its competitors, Magellan and WebCrawler. These continue to run as separate services.

AOL NetFind is a branded version of the Excite search engine in North America.

Main features that affect Web page design
(as of August 1998)

Total Web Pages in index	55 million
Pages crawled per day	3 million
Time for submitted pages to be indexed	1 to 3 weeks
Time for unsubmitted pages	3 weeks
Frames support	No
Image map support	No
Ranks link popularity	Yes
Ranks meta tags	No
Indexes image Alt text	No
Indexes comments	No
Case sensitive	No
Maximum title length	70 characters
Maximum description length	395 characters
Meta tag display support	No
Shows last modified date	No

HotBot / Inktomi:

http://www.hotbot.com/

Launched in May 1996, HotBot is Wired Digital's entry into the search engine market. The site is powered by the Inktomi search engine, which is also used by other services, such as GoTo.com.

It has a partnership with LookSmart for its directory listings.

Linked at the bottom of a Yahoo search page, so is likely to be used if Yahoo (the most popular search tool) fails to find a match.

Main features that affect Web page design
(as of August 1998)

Total Web Pages in index	110 million
Pages crawled per day	Up to 10 million
Time for submitted pages to be indexed	Up to 2 weeks
Time for unsubmitted pages	2 weeks
Frames support	No
Image map support	No
Ranks link popularity	No
Ranks meta tags	Yes
Indexes image Alt text	No
Indexes comments	Yes
Case sensitive	Mixed
Maximum title length	115 characters
Maximum description length	249 characters
Meta tag display support	Yes
Shows last modified date	Yes

Infoseek:

http://www.infoseek.com/

Around since early 1995, Infoseek is well-known, well-reviewed and well-connected. In late 1996, a new service with 30 million URLs was introduced and listing a site took only minutes. Times have changed since May 1998 and it now takes up to 2 days.

Infoseek also runs a directory separate from its search engine.

Linked at the bottom of a Yahoo search page, so is likely to be used if Yahoo (the most popular search tool) fails to find a match.

Main features that affect Web page design
(as of August 1998)

Total Web Pages in index	30 million
Pages crawled per day	Not known
Time for submitted pages to be indexed	Up to 2 days
Time for unsubmitted pages	1 to 2 months
Frames support	No
Image map support	Yes
Ranks link popularity	Yes
Ranks meta tags	Yes
Indexes image Alt text	Yes
Indexes comments	No
Case sensitive	Yes
Maximum title length	70 characters
Maximum description length	240 characters
Meta tag display support	Yes
Shows last modified date	Yes

Lycos:

Around since May 1994, Lycos is one of the oldest of the major search engines. It began as a project at Carnegie Mellon University. The name Lycos comes from the Latin for "wolf spider." Lycos operates for AOL NetFind in Europe.

Lycos lists sites in two main ways. There are search engine listings, and there is an associated directory called "Community Guides."

Linked at the bottom of a Yahoo search page, so is likely to be used if Yahoo (the most popular search tool) fails to find a match.

Main features that affect Web page design
(as of August 1998)

Total Web Pages in index	30 million
Pages crawled per day	6 to 10 million
Time for submitted pages to be indexed	2 to 3 weeks
Time for unsubmitted pages	2 to 3 weeks
Frames support	No
Image map support	No
Ranks link popularity	Yes
Ranks meta tags	No
Indexes image Alt text	Yes
Indexes comments	No
Case sensitive	No
Maximum title length	60 characters
Maximum description length	200 characters
Meta tag display support	No
Shows last modified date	No

Northern Light:

http://www.northernlight.com/
http://www.nlsearch.com/

Northern Light opened to general use in August 1997. While it doesn't have the strategic alliances of the other major search engines, it is seriously crawling significant portions of the web and thus qualifies to be among the major search engines. Northern Light features an ability to classify documents by topic, which it hopes will distinguish it from some of the other search services, even those with their own topical listings.

Main features that affect Web page design
(as of August 1998)

Total Web Pages in index	80 million
Pages crawled per day	3+ million
Time for submitted pages to be indexed	2 to 4 weeks
Time for unsubmitted pages	2 to 4 weeks
Frames support	Yes
Image map support	Yes
Ranks link popularity	No
Ranks meta tags	No
Indexes image Alt text	No
Indexes comments	No
Case sensitive	Mixed
Maximum title length	80 characters
Maximum description length	200 characters
Meta tag display support	No
Shows last modified date	Yes

WebCrawler:

http://www.webcrawler.com/

WebCrawler opened to the public in April 1994. It was started as a research project at the University of Washington. In November 1966 Excite acquired the service and runs WebCrawler as an independent search engine.

Linked at the bottom of a Yahoo search page, so is likely to be used if Yahoo (the most popular search tool) fails to find a match.

Main features that affect Web page design
(as of August 1998)

Total Web Pages in index	2 million
Pages crawled per day	Not known
Time for submitted pages to be indexed	1 to 6 weeks
Time for unsubmitted pages	Unlikely
Frames support	No
Image map support	Yes
Ranks link popularity	Yes
Ranks meta tags	No
Indexes image Alt text	No
Indexes comments	No
Case sensitive	No
Maximum title length	60 characters
Maximum description length	395 characters
Meta tag display support	No
Shows last modified date	No

Yahoo:

http://www.yahoo.com/

Around since late 1994, Yahoo is the oldest major web site directory. Yahoo is well-known, well-used and well-respected. It is also the largest directory (as opposed to search engine), listing 750,000 web sites, as of December 1997. Because Yahoo is a directory, based on user submissions, it may not list some sites that a crawler might find from searching the web each day. If a search of Yahoo doesn't turn up any useful links, you should try a search engine. Yahoo makes this easy to do, as the query originally sent to Yahoo is forwarded to any of the major search engines linked at the bottom of each results page.

Yahoo is not always easy to get listed on.

LookSmart:

http://www.looksmart.com/

LookSmart was launched in October 1996. It is the closest rival Yahoo has, in terms of a human-compiled directory. It listed about 300,000 web sites as of February 1998.

LookSmart was positioned on the Netscape Net Search page and also provides browsable listings for both AltaVista and HotBot.

AltaVista provides LookSmart with search results when a search fails to find a match from among LookSmart's reviews.

Microsoft Start

http://home.microsoft.com/

Microsoft announced in October 1997 that it was partnering with Inktomi to create a search engine for its Internet Start page. Currently, that search service has yet to appear. At the moment, Internet Start features web searching through other companies.

Netscape Netcenter

http://home.netscape.com/

Netscape shifted its strategy in Spring 1998 to compete as a portal site. Its old site has been replaced with Netcenter which caters for both search and navigation. Most of this content is repackaged by Netscape's partner, Excite, who also power Netscape's search engine. Netscape also offers an option to use other companies' search engines.

AOL Netfind

http://www.aol.com/netfind/

Galaxy

http://www.einet.net/

GoTo

http://www.goto.com/

NetGuide

http://www.netguide.com/

PlanetSearch

http://www.planetsearch.com/

Snap!

http://www.snap.com/

Design Tips

We include here details of some of the tips and techniques that may help to get your Web pages a little higher up the search engine rankings.

Choosing Keywords:

The words you imagine your future 'customers' typing into a search engine should be your site keywords. Some important things to remember when picking keywords for your site may include:

Concepts - Include concept keywords such as 'landscape paintings' if that's what you sell, but also try and be specific enough so that its not too broad.

Brandnames - Try and include specific brand names that are easily recognisable. Obviously they have to be relevant to the site though. Legally, you should put the ® reserved symbol or ™ trademark symbol after the names when mentioning them on the page.

Company Names - Similarly if you offer products from a well known company, include that company's name in your keywords.

Stop Words - There are now so many pages and words indexed on the Web, that a search on many common words (such as 'and', 'the' or 'Internet') is simply ignored by the search engines. These are called stop words.

Phrases - Many people will search using two-word or three-word phrases to find what they're looking for, so you should try to include as many phrase keyword combinations as you can. When placing keywords on your page, try to include them in a phrase that visitors might use and keep the important words chained together in sentences on the page. Optimising your page for phrase searches can do wonders in helping people find you.

Stemming - This is whether a search engine will also search for variations of a word based on its stem. For example, if you developed a Web site concerning mutual funds, you might use keywords like invest, invests, investment, and investor. Infoseek, Lycos and Northern Light carry out stemming searches, so this would not be necessary, but the other engines don't.

Case-Sensitivity - If a user searches on the word Football, then most engines will search for 'Football' with an uppercase 'F'. If your page has only 'football' in it, you will not be found! But, if they search for 'football' and your page contains the keyword 'Football', you may be luckier, as most engines default to finding words of any case when the search-word used was in all lower case. It may pay to make sure you have at least some of the keywords in uppercase or starting with an uppercase letter. Some people, in fact, include all their meta tag keywords in upper case.

Spelling - Other people's spelling may not be as good as yours and search engines don't have spell checkers. It sometimes pays to think of obvious spelling mistakes that people are likely to make when entering their search requests, and include these as keywords. This way you may pick up some traffic you would otherwise miss.

Placing Keywords on your Page:

Earlier in the chapter we discussed how search engines rank sites in their search results. The position of your keywords is essential here. When the keywords appear in the page title they are considered more relevant and given a higher weighting. Next, if they appear near the top of a page, such as in the heading or in the first few paragraphs of text they also carry more weight.

Be careful that tables or sections of Javascript do not 'push' your keyworded text lower down your page than you expect. This may lower your ranking.

Using Meta Tags:

As we saw earlier, Meta tags can help you control your site's description in the search results of the engines that support them. You must use meta tags then, but do not expect them to actually raise your ranking position too much. As most people browse the descriptions from a search listing first, a well prepared one using meta tags must have a better chance of being accessed than some we have seen.

Submitting to Search Engines

Once you are happy that your site is fully complete and that you have your pages fully optimised for higher search engine placement, you can get ready to start submitting your site. If you do this too early it can be a problem to get some of the search engines and directories to change their listings if you later decide on major improvements.

You should hand submit the details of your site at least to all the major search engines we listed earlier in the chapter. There are many more search and directory sites that you could also get listed on. Doing this all by hand can be an arduous and boring task and it is possible to use a multi-submit site to do it for you, like Submit It!, one of the original submission services.

http://www.submit-it.com/

When you do something yourself though, at least you know who was doing the job and whether it was done properly. So it might be good policy to only use multi-submit sites as a last resort.

An Initial Data File:

When you submit details to search engines you will be asked to complete a form with your site details. Some only ask for the URL, but others expect you to send a lot of information. It is worth spending an hour at this stage getting the likely information that will be needed into one place. We use a Notepad file to store our personal and site data and keep it open so that we can cut and paste data from it into the form being completed.

This not only saves a lot of time actually typing and looking for things, but it is much harder to enter incorrect data this way. Submitting a wrong URL or e-mail address can be fatal here.

We suggest your file should contain the following data, double-spaced for easier copying to the clipboard:

Name

Home address

Business address, if different

County, state or province

Country

Phone and fax numbers - home

Phone and fax numbers - business

URL of the site

e-mail address

All the site keywords on one line

The most important five keywords on one line

Three site descriptions as follows:
Remember to use as many of your main keywords as possible in all these as they may be used to rank your site.

A 160 character description to use at Yahoo and other directories.

A 25 word short description of the site

A 50 word description.

If you are asked anything else during the submission process you can add it to your file as you go along.

Adding your URL:

Pretty well all search engines allow you to add your URLs to their database for spidering. You are only supposed to submit the URL of your site home page, but many people register at least all the key pages of their site.

Once you have accessed the home page of the search engine, look for a link called something like 'Add URL'. This is usually at the top or bottom of the page. If you can't see one, you may have to browse through their Help pages. Once found, you can go to their URL Submission page and follow their instructions, with the help of your prepared data file.

Before leaving each submission page we suggest you do the following.

1   Add a bookmark of the page to your browser. We keep a special bookmark folder to hold these links for future use.

2   Make a note of everything you did and when. A detailed log of your search engine submissions can help you analyse how successful you have been.

All you do then is work through our list!

The procedure at Yahoo! is a little different. Remember that this is a directory, not a search engine and one of their editors (a live human being) will actually visit and evaluate your site. Yahoo listings are somewhat harder to get, but they can be very important, as it is a very popular search tool.

The Yahoo site is organised as a huge directory listing with hundreds of categories. Before contacting them you should explore this directory and find the page that best fits your particular site. From this page click the 'Add URL' button and follow their instructions. If you are lucky you will be contacted within a few days by one of their editors to give details of your entry. Don't be too surprised though, to find you have been placed on a different page. If you object to this, at least you should have a name and e-mail address of the person to contact. The whole system works well for us, but it took many months and many attempts, before we were successful.

Checking your Entries:

In the following few weeks you will need to check that the search engines have indexed your site. Remember that in some cases the procedure can take many weeks. We have given an indication of the likely waiting time in our listing of the major search engines.

You can easily do this manually, but 'Submit It! Verifier' is a free tool that can help you with the process. The URL to download this, is at:

http://www.submit-it.com/verify/SIVerExample.cfm

While we are on the subject of free tools, another one you may find useful is 'Position Agent'. This can help you check the ranking your particular URL occupies for a given search engine query.

http://www.positionagent.com/free.htm

Reciprocal Links

The more places on the Web that have links back to your site the more likely you are to get visitors, so you should find sites which will attract the type of visitors you're looking for on your own site. If you are not a direct competitor, you could e-mail the Webmaster of these related sites and ask them if they will add a link to your site if you add a link to theirs. Successfully negotiating a link from another well placed site can do wonders for improving quality traffic to your own site.

There are many ways of finding good sites to try and link with. Perhaps the best is to search with different search engines using the keywords that you think best fit the ones you have built into your own site. The ones that come up towards the top of the lists are prime candidates. They will be getting the type of viewers you are looking for.

Visit their sites and if they still look suitable send a friendly e-mail request to the Webmaster whose e-mail details should be given at the bottom of the home page. It might pay to say something complimentary and relevant about his or her site. If a link is agreed to, make sure you send a thank you message when it is all installed.

Bruce Clay has produced an excellent and very detailed Web page on this subject, located at:

http://www.bruceclay.com/web_rank.htm

You may find it a good idea to have a special part of your site put aside to hold all your reciprocal links. If you are a busy bee and get several hundred of them, you can make this section into quite a feature of your site. You will get quite a lot of traffic this way and you should increase you search engine rankings as well!

Other Ways to Promote your Site

Although being indexed well on the major search engines is the number one thing you can do to promote your site inexpensively, there are other effective ways.

Banner ads:

You see them all over the Web. On average about 3 or 4 people click them for every 100 times a banner is displayed. We must admit that we hardly ever do! They can be cost effective if you use an eye catching design and slogan and you TARGET your message. Try to advertise on sites that are related to your target audience. Most of the search engines now let you display banners based on the keyword the user is searching on, but at a cost.

If your budget is tight, however, consider a free banner exchange service such as LinkExchange:

http://www.linkexchange.com/

For every two banner impressions you allow to be displayed on your site, they will display your banner on another site free of charge. It's all automated and can increase your traffic with no cost. However, there are drawbacks such as the risk of losing your own customers prematurely if they chase after someone else's advertisement. Also, banners can increase the loading time of your page somewhat. Still, it may be worth thinking about.

Free Offers:

This one is used all over the Web as well and can work if you have an interesting product to give away. Combine this technique with another to be effective, as you still need to let people know about your site.

Newsgroups:

Get in the habit of paying regular visits to newsgroups that your target audience are likely to frequent. Leave helpful messages and sign your message with a signature describing your Web site, product or services. Be careful not to sound too much like a sales pitch though, or you'll violate the rules of many newsgroups.

E-mail:

E-mail is a powerful sales tool, but avoid sending unsolicited and untargetted e-mails. You'll get far more hostile and negative responses than positive ones. Use e-mail for follow up and when people have asked to be put on a list, or to receive information.

Signature file:

An opportunity that many overlook is to put their Web site URL into their signature file for e-mail and Newsgroup postings. Make sure you write it out in full, with the preceding http:// as some mailreaders now recognise URLs and automatically make them into links. With no cut and paste involved, people are more likely to just click and have a look at your site.

Newsletters:

If you have good writing skills, you could write a free newsletter about the subject area you are targeting and send it by e-mail to subscribers. Make the content fresh and interesting and you could build a large following in no time, but it is hard work.

Content:

Don't forget to put in at least as much effort into the actual content and design of your site as you do in the promotion. Otherwise, you may get people to your site but few will take advantage of your product or service. If your site content changes frequently or is re-usable in some way, it can work to draw people back for repeat visits. However, this does not always happen so at least try and capture the user's name in order to follow up with a friendly e-mail or special offer later. You should always make it easy to contact you in whatever way they choose. We also have a guest book for this purpose.

Off-Line Promotion

Just because your Web site is on the Internet does not mean you are confined to that medium for your promotion efforts. Some of the following methods should be very successful at letting people know about your site. But not many of them are free.

Press Releases:

Traditional type press releases can work wonders for site traffic if your release is picked up and published in a magazine or newspaper. Try and target the type of papers that your users are likely to read, but at the end of the day any coverage is good coverage. This one can be very powerful - don't ignore it.

Advertisements:

If you can't persuade press editors to give you free publicity it may be worth while paying for an advertisement or two. In any case make sure that any advertising your organisation does includes your Web site address. This is where domain names come into their own. We have seen URLs recently on television, the sides of boats, buses, balloons, product packaging, roadside hoardings and at almost every sports venue possible.

Stationery:

Put your URL everywhere you possibly can - on letterheads, faxes, business cards, invoices, promotional items, even your voice mail, if you believe in the horrible concept.

One cheap and very effective way of promoting your site is to have a postcard printed with a relevant picture on one side and a prominent URL on the other. Don't forget the Christmas cards you were going to get printed!

Get the URL Right:

The most important thing is to be sure that the printer uses the correct URL and doesn't insert spurious spaces, or make stops into commas, or the colon into a semicolon. Most people leave off the ending /, but it is actually correct to provide it. Proof reading is essential here.

10. MAINTAINING YOUR WEB SITE

Once your site is built, placed on the server and listed on most of the search engines, your job is finished and you can sit back and relax. Right? Maybe for a day or two, but to be successful you cannot rest on your laurels in the Web business.

There is a steady string of action required to maintain your site, to keep it up to date and to keep its position in the search rankings. If you just let it look after itself it will very soon become dated and, worse, it will fall out of the search listings.

Maintaining Search Rankings

As we saw in the last chapter, it takes a lot of effort to get a site to a good position in the search lists, and without this good position it will not receive the number of visitors it should. Well, it takes as much work keeping it there!

You should make an effort to be continuously adding to your site and making useful changes. This will not only make it more interesting for repeat visitors, but will encourage the search engine spiders to keep updating the site. This helps to maintain your ranking. An unchanged site will be spidered less and less and with the huge numbers of new sites being added all the time to compete with, will get submerged.

To help with this you should get in the habit of checking your ranking with all the search engines every week or two. It often happens that a site will suddenly drop out of them for some unexplained reason. No one else will tell you if this happens, so you must keep track yourself. If this does happen to you, you must start the listing process again, but first have a look at the frequency of your keywords. In the battle against spammers the search engines seem to be always changing their rules these days. You may have too many keywords and have been penalised.

The stakes are high and your competitors all round the globe will be trying to get their sites to appear on the first page of the search listings, so be prepared for 'battle'.

Counting Visitors:

If you want to know how many visitors your Web pages are getting you will need to organise a way of obtaining site statistics. This should be where your service provider or host server administration comes in. Most servers will have some way of providing details of access statistics for the sites on their books. If you are lucky, these will provide complete details of each visit including for example, the time of visit, who visited, the type of browser they were using, where they came from, how long they stayed and what pages they looked at. All of these are provided automatically by you accessing a specific URL. At the other end of the scale, you may only get access to a counter which requires you to add some HTML code to your page before it will work.

Ask your system administrator if they offer access statistics and get full details of how to use the service. If you have no luck in this direction all is not lost, but you will have to do some more work of your own. A search for 'access counters' on one of the main engines, such as AltVista, should provide many venues for you to follow.

There are many services that provide free counters you can add to your pages in exchange for a banner advert. Some of these banners can be very ugly, but some are OK. We have even found some that let you make the banner invisible, but you have to dig into their instruction pages. Also, you can get a very good statistical service from many places if you are prepared to pay a pound or two a month.

Another alternative, if you can turn your hand to a little 'programming' is to get a Perl CGI Script, maybe from Matt Wright at:

http://www.worldwidemart.com/mattw/

He writes books on the subject and runs the Web site as a gateway service. Well worth a visit if you want to improve your skills and add a lot of customised features to your site. But completely outside the scope of this book!

Keeping Things up to Date

As we saw, this entails making continuous changes to your site. On the Web, six months is a long time and a site that has not been updated over such a period may not be considered by some to be topical. Obviously this will depend on what type of site you run. The history of ancient Greece, for example, does not change very much these days, but maybe the way it is presented can.

One thing to remember is to keep the details of the date that the site was last maintained up to date on your pages. It is easy to open a page, make a few changes and send the page to your server without bothering to go to the bottom and change the date.

Checking Links:

You should get into the habit of checking all the links on your site every few weeks. The links to external sites especially, are vulnerable here. Sites close down, or move servers without leaving a forwarding address, and when you try to access them, you get a dreadful 'URL Not Found' type message screen. Try to keep these away from your site.

One problem we had was with other people's banner links. To save on our server space, we linked to a lot of other art sites by showing their banners, but leaving the actual graphic files for these on their servers. This worked well for a while, but we had no control over the other sites. When they made a change to their site structure, or used another banner, our site would no longer be able to find the graphic and we had an embarrassing hole on our page. Now we store all these banner graphic files on our own server!

Domain Names:

If you have your own domain name, like michaelstrang.com for example, it may be wise to obtain a trademark registration for it. There has been a lot of fuss lately about unscrupulous operators registering domain names similar to those of well known organisations and trying to profit from them.

You should check your domain name record to be sure that your registration authority has correctly listed who owns your domain name. Make sure it lists up-to-date postal, e-mail, and telephone contact information for you. If not get it changed.

Finally, if your registration authority (e.g. Internic for .com domains) charges maintenance fees, then you should make a note of when they are next due, in case you do not receive a reminder. We have known people who have forgotten this and suddenly lost their domain name. Be warned.

Well that's it. We hope you have enjoyed reading this as much as we have enjoyed writing it. A glossary is included next, for reference, and in case you have trouble with any jargon that may have crept in.

11. GLOSSARY OF TERMS

Add-in
: A mini-program which runs in conjunction with a web browser and enhances its functionality.

Address
: A unique number or name that identifies a specific computer or user on a network.

Agent
: A search tool that automatically seeks out relevant on-line information.

Anonymous FTP
: Anonymous FTP allows you to connect to a remote computer and transfer public files back to your local computer without the need to have a user ID and password.

Application
: Software (program) designed to carry out certain activity, such as word processing.

Applet
: A program that can be downloaded over a network and launched on the user's computer.

Archie
: Archie is an Internet service that allows you to locate files that can be downloaded via FTP.

Association
: An identification of a filename extension to a program. This lets Windows open the program when its files are selected.

ASCII
: A binary code representation of a character set. The name stands for 'American Standard Code for Information Interchange'.

Attribute	A setting for an HTML tag, that affects the way the tag is rendered.
Authoring	The process of creating web documents or software.
Backbone	The main transmission lines of the Internet, running at over 45Mbps.
Backup	To make a back-up copy of a file or a disc for safekeeping.
Bandwidth	The range of transmission frequencies a network can use. The greater the bandwidth the more information that can be transferred over a network.
Banner	An advertising graphic shown on a Web page.
Baud	The unit of measurement used to describe data transmission speed. One baud is one bit per second.
BBS	Bulletin Board System, a computer equipped with software and telecoms links that allow it to act as an information host for remote computer systems.
BinHex	A file conversion format that converts binary files to ASCII text files.
BIOS	The Basic Input/Output System. It allows the core of a PC's operating system to communicate with the hardware.
Bit	A binary digit; the smallest unit of information that can be stored, either as a 1 or as a 0.

Bitmap	A technique for managing the image displayed on a computer screen.
Bookmarks	A list of 'favourite' places used for quick access from a browser.
Browse	A button in some Windows dialogue boxes that lets you view a list of files and folders before you make a selection.
Browser	A program, like the Internet Explorer, that lets you graphically view Web pages.
Buffer	RAM memory allocated to store data being read from disc.
Byte	A grouping of binary digits (0 or 1) which represent information.
Cache	An area of memory, or disc space, reserved for data, which speeds up down-loading.
Card	A removable printed-circuit board that is plugged into a computer expansion slot.
CD-ROM	Compact Disc - Read Only Memory; an optical disc which information may be read from but not written to.
CGI	Common Gateway Interface - a convention for servers to communicate with local applications and allow users to provide information to scripts attached to web pages, usually through forms.

cgi-bin	The most common name of a directory on a web server in which CGI programs are stored.
Chat	A system that allows for on-line communication between Internet users.
Check box	A small box in a dialogue box that can be selected (X), or cleared (empty).
Client	A computer that has access to services over a computer network. The computer providing the services is a server.
Client application	A Windows application that can accept linked, or embedded, objects.
Clipboard	A temporary storage area of memory, where text and graphics are stored with the Windows cut and copy actions.
Command	An instruction given to a computer to carry out a particular action.
Command line	The line in an MS-DOS window, or screen, into which you enter DOS commands.
Compressed files	One that is compacted to save server space and reduce transfer times. Typical file extensions for compressed files include zip (DOS/Windows) and tar (UNIX).
Configuration	A general purpose term referring to the way you have your computer set up.

Cookies	Files stored on your hard drive by your Web browser that hold information for it to use.
Counter	A number on many web pages that will count the number of visits to the page.
CPU	The Central Processing Unit; the main chip that executes all instructions entered into a computer.
Cybercafe	Establishment with both coffee and Internet access for sale.
Cyberspace	Originated by William Gibson in his novel 'Neuromancer', now used to describe the Internet and the other computer networks.
Dial-up Connection	A popular form of Net connection for the home user, over standard telephone lines.
Direct Connection	A permanent connection between your computer system and the Internet.
Default	The command, device or option automatically chosen.
Desktop	The Windows screen working background, on which you place icons, folders, etc.
Device driver	A special file that must be loaded into memory for Windows to be able to address a specific procedure or hardware device.
Device name	A logical name used by DOS to identify a device, such as LPT1 or COM1 for the parallel or serial printer.

Dialogue box	A window displayed on the screen to allow the user to enter information.
Directory	An area on disc where information relating to a group of files is kept. Known as a folder in Windows 95.
Disc	A device on which you can store programs and data.
Disconnect	To detach a drive, port or computer from a shared device, or to break an Internet connection.
Document	When used in reference to the Web, a document is any file containing text, media or hyperlinks that can be transferred from an HTTP server to a browser. Otherwise it is a file produced by an application program.
Domain	A group of devices, servers and computers on a network.
Domain Name	The name of an Internet site, for example www.michaelstrang.com, which allows you to reference Internet sites without knowing their true numerical address.
DOS	Disc Operating System. A collection of small specialised programs that allow interaction between user and computer.
Double-click	To quickly press and release a mouse button twice.
Download	To transfer to your computer a file, or data, from another computer.

DPI	Dots Per Inch - a resolution standard for laser printers.
Drag	To move an object on the screen by pressing and holding down the left mouse button while moving the mouse.
Drive name	The letter followed by a colon which identifies a floppy or hard disc drive.
EISA	Extended Industry Standard Architecture, for construction of PCs with the Intel 32-bit micro-processor.
Embedded object	Information in a document that is 'copied' from its source application. Selecting the object opens the creating application from within the document.
Engine	Software used by search services.
E-mail	Electronic Mail - A system that allows computer users to send and receive messages electronically.
Ethernet	A very common method of networking computers in a LAN.
Expanded memory	This is memory outside the conventional RAM (first 640 KB) and is used by some MS-DOS software to store data and run applications.
Extended memory	This is memory above the 1-MB memory address, all of which is used by Windows 95.
FAQ	Frequently Asked Questions - A common feature on the Internet,

145

	FAQs are files of answers to commonly asked questions.
FAT	The File Allocation Table. An area on disc where information is kept on which part of the disc a file is located.
File extension	The optional suffix following the period in a filename. Windows uses this to identify the source application program.
Filename	The name given to a file. In Windows 95 this can be up to 256 characters long.
Filespec	File specification made up of drive, path and filename.
Firewall	Security measures designed to protect a networked system from unauthorised access.
Floppy disc	A removable disc on which information can be stored magnetically.
Folder	An area used to store a group of files, usually with a common link.
Flame	An insulting message exchanged via e-mail or within newsgroups.
Font	A graphic design representing a set of characters, numbers and symbols.
Form	An HTML tag providing 'graphical user interface' elements allowing users to interact with CGI services via forms.
Frame	An HTML tag introduced by Netscape to allow partitioning of the browser window into

	independent document display areas.
Freeware	Software that is available for downloading and unlimited use without charge.
FTP	File Transfer Protocol. The procedure for connecting to a remote computer and transferring files.
Function key	One of the series of 10 or 12 keys marked with the letter F and a numeral, used for specific operations.
Gateway	A computer system that allows otherwise incompatible networks to communicate with each other.
GIF	Graphics Interchange Format, a common standard for images on the Web.
Gopher	A text oriented, hierarchically organised, tool used to locate on-line resources.
Graphic	A picture or illustration, also called an image. Formats include GIF, JPEG, BMP, PCX, and TIFF.
Graphics card	A device that controls the display on the monitor and other allied functions.
GUI	A Graphic User Interface, such as Windows 98, the software front-end meant to provide an attractive and easy to use interface.
Hardcopy	Output on paper.

Hard disc	A device built into the computer for holding programs and data.
Hardware	The equipment that makes up a computer system, excluding the programs or software.
Help	A Windows system that gives you instructions and additional information on using a program.
Helper application	A program allowing you to view multimedia files that your web browser cannot handle internally.
Hit	A single request from a web browser for a single item from a web server.
Home page	The document displayed when you first open your Web browser, or the first document you come to at a Web site.
Host	Computer connected directly to the Internet that provides services to other local and/or remote computers.
Hot Java	A Web browser developed by Sun Microsystems that takes full advantage of applets written in the Java programming language.
Hotlist	A list of frequently used Web locations and URL addresses.
Host	A computer acting as an information or communications server.
HTML	HyperText Markup Language, the format used in documents on the Web.

HTML editor	Authoring tool which assists with the creation of HTML pages.
HTTP	HyperText Transport Protocol, the system used to link and transfer hypertext documents on the Web.
Hyperlink	A segment of text, or an inline image, that refers to another document on the Web.
Hypermedia	Hypertext extended to include linked multi-media.
Hypertext	A system that allows documents to be cross-linked so that the reader can explore related links, or documents, by clicking on a highlighted word or symbol.
Icon	A small graphic image that represents a function or object. Clicking on an icon produces an action.
Image	See graphic.
Imagemap	An image which has specified areas hyperlinked to some other page or service.
Indexing	The process of analysing Web pages and recording the occurrences of keywords for later use by search engines.
Insertion point	A flashing bar that shows where typed text will be entered into a document.
Interface	A device that allows you to connect a computer to its peripherals.
Internet	The global system of computer networks.

Intranet	A private network inside an organisation using the same kind of software as the Internet.
IRC	Internet Relay Chat - World-wide real-time conferencing on the Internet.
IRQ	Interrupt request lines - hardware lines used by devices to signal the processor that they are ready to send, or receive, data.
ISA	Industry Standard Architecture; a standard for internal connections in PCs.
ISDN	Integrated Services Digital Network, a telecom standard using digital transmission technology to support voice, video and data communications applications over regular telephone lines.
IP	Internet Protocol - The rules that provide basic Internet functions.
IP Address	Internet Protocol Address - every computer on the Internet has a unique identifying number.
ISP	Internet Service Provider - A company that offers access to the Internet.
Java	An object-oriented programming language created by Sun Microsystems for developing applets that are capable of running on any computer, regardless of the operating system.

JPEG /JPG	Joint Photographic Experts Group, a popular cross-platform format for image files. JPEG is best suited for truecolor original images.
Keyword	A searchable term which can be extracted from a data set, such as a Web page, during indexing.
Kilobyte	(KB); 1024 bytes of information or storage space.
LAN	Local Area Network - High-speed, privately-owned network covering a limited geographical area, such as an office or a building.
Laptop	A portable computer small enough to sit on your lap.
LCD	Liquid Crystal Display.
Leased-line	A leased phone line that provides a dedicated, direct connection to the Internet.
Links	The hypertext connections between Web pages.
Local	A resource that is located on your computer, not linked to it over a network.
Location	An Internet address.
Log on	To gain access to a network.
Markup	Syntactically delimited characters added to the data of a document to represent its structure.
MCI	Media Control Interface - a standard for files and multi-media devices.

Megabyte	(MB); 1024 kilobytes of information or storage space.
Megahertz	(MHz); Speed of processor in millions of cycles per second.
Memory	Part of computer consisting of storage elements organised into addressable locations that can hold data and instructions.
Menu	A list of available options in an application.
Menu bar	The horizontal bar that lists the names of menus.
Microprocessor	The calculating chip within a computer.
Microsoft	The world's largest operating system and application software development company. Home of Bill Gates.
MIDI	Musical Instrument Digital Interface - enables devices to transmit and receive sound and music messages.
MIME	Multipurpose Internet Mail Extensions, a messaging standard that allows Internet users to exchange e-mail messages enhanced with graphics, video and voice.
MIPS	Million Instructions Per Second; measures speed of a system.
Mirror Site	An Internet site set up as an alternate to a busy site; contains copies of all the files stored at the primary location.

Meta	An HTML tag used in the Head area of a document to specify further information about the document.
Metasearcher	A search engine that simultaneously passes a user's query on to several other search engines in parallel.
Modem	Short for Modulator-demodulator devices. An electronic device that lets computers communicate electronically.
Monitor	The display device connected to your PC, also called a screen.
Mouse	A device used to manipulate a pointer around your display and activate processes by pressing buttons.
Mouse Potato	Those of us who spend too much time in front of the computer. Recently included in the Oxford English Dictionary.
Mozilla	Alias for the Netscape browser.
MPEG	Motion Picture Experts Group - a video file format offering excellent quality in a relatively small file.
MS-DOS	Microsoft's implementation of the Disc Operating System for PCs.
Multimedia	The use of photographs, music and sound and movie images in a presentation.
Multi-tasking	Performing more than one operation at the same time.

NCSA	National Center for Super-computing Applications. A US federal funded organisation for the R and D of high-technology resources.
Netscape	A popular browser manufacturer.
Network	Two or more computers connected together to share resources.
Network server	Central computer which stores files for several linked computers.
NNTP	Network News Transfer Protocol A common method of article transfer over Usenet.
Node	Any single computer connected to a network.
Online	Having access to the Internet.
On-line Service	Services such as America On-line and CompuServe that provide content to subscribers and usually connections to the Internet.
Operating system	Software that runs a computer.
Packet	A piece of data. The TCP/IP protocol breaks large data files into smaller "packets" for transmission.
Page	An HTML document, or Web site.
Password	A unique character string used to gain access to a network, program, or mailbox.
PATH	The location of a file in the directory tree.
Peripheral	Any device attached to a PC.

Perl	A popular language for programming CGI applications.
PIF file	Program information file - gives information to Windows about an MS-DOS application.
PING	A program for determining if another computer is currently connected to the Internet.
Pixel	A picture element on screen; the smallest element that can be independently assigned colour and intensity.
PKZIP	A widely available shareware utility allowing users to compress and decompress data files.
Plug-and-play	Hardware which can be plugged into a PC and be used immediately without configuration.
Plugin	A helper application that runs within a Web browser, used to display data types that the browser cannot handle internally.
PNG	Portable Network Graphics, an extensible file format for the lossless, portable, compressed storage of raster images. PNG provides a patent-free replacement for the GIF format.
POP	Post Office Protocol - a method of storing and returning e-mail.
Port	The place where information goes into or out of a computer. E.g. a modem might be connected to the serial port. With the Internet, port often refers to a number that is part of a URL.

Post	To send a message to a mailing list or newsgroup.
PPP	Point-to-Point Protocol - One of two methods (see SLIP) for using special software to establish a temporary direct connection to the Internet over regular phone lines.
Print queue	A list of print jobs waiting to be sent to a printer.
Program	A set of instructions which cause a computer to perform tasks.
Promotion	Informing the world of the presence of your Web site.
Protocol	A set of rules or standards that define how computers commun-icate with each other.
Push	Automatically update info on your computer when you log onto the Internet.
Query	The set of keywords and operators sent by a user to a search engine.
Queue	A list of e-mail messages waiting to be sent over the Internet.
RAM	Random Access Memory. The computer's volatile memory. Data held in it is lost when power is switched off.
Real mode	MS-DOS mode, typically used to run programs, such as MS-DOS games, that will not run under Windows.
Register	To contact the supplier of soft-ware that you have purchased to give your personal details.

Resource	A directory, or printer, that can be shared over a network.
Robot	A Web agent that visits sites, by requesting documents from them, for the purposes of indexing for search engines. Also known as Wanderers, Crawlers, or Spiders.
ROM	Read Only Memory. A PC's non-volatile memory. Data is written into this memory at manufacture and is not affected by power loss.
Router	A communications device used to transmit over a network via the most efficient route possible.
Screen saver	A display program that moves images on an inactive screen.
Scroll bar	A bar that appears at the right side or bottom edge of a window.
Search	Submit a query to a search engine.
Search engine	A program that helps users find information across the Internet.
Serial interface	An interface that transfers data as individual bits.
Server	A computer system that manages and delivers information for client computers.
SGML	Standard Generalised Markup Language. An SGML document consists of data characters and markup; the markup describes the structure of the information and an instance of that structure.

Shared resource	Any device, program or file that is available to network users.
Shareware	Software that is available on public networks and bulletin boards. Users are expected to pay a nominal amount to the software developer.
Signature file	An ASCII text file, maintained within e-mail programs, that contains text for your signature.
Site	A place on the Internet. Every Web page has a location where it resides which is called its site.
SLIP	Serial Line Internet Protocol, a method of Internet connection that enables computers to use phone lines and a modem to connect to the Internet without having to connect to a host.
SMTP	Simple Mail Transfer Protocol - a protocol dictating how e-mail messages are exchanged over the Internet.
Snail mail	Ordinary paper mail sent through a post office.
Socket	An end-point for sending and receiving data between computers.
Software	The programs and instructions that control your PC.
Spamming	Sending the same message to a large number of mailing lists or newsgroups. Also to overload a Web page with excessive keywords in an attempt to get a better search ranking.

Spider	See robot.
Spooler	Software which handles transfer of information to a store to be used by a peripheral device.
SQL	Structured Query Language, used with relational databases.
SSL	Secure Sockets Layer, the standard transmission security protocol developed by Netscape, which has been put into the public domain.
Subscribe	To become of a member of.
Surfing	The process of looking around the Internet.
SVGA	Super Video Graphics Array; it has all the VGA modes but with 256, or more, colours.
Swap file	An area of your hard disc used to store temporary operating files, also known as virtual memory.
Sysop	System Operator - A person responsible for the physical operations of a computer system or network resource.
System disc	A disc containing files to enable a PC to start up.
T1	An Internet leased line that carries up to 1.536 million bits per second (1.536Mbps).
T3	An Internet leased line that carries up to 45 million bits per second (45Mbps).
Table	An HTML tag used for element layout.

Tag	Markup that delimits an HTML element. A tag includes a name which refers to an element declaration and can include attributes.
TCP/IP	Transmission Control Protocol/ Internet Protocol, combined protocols that perform the transfer of data between two computers. TCP monitors and ensures the correct transfer of data. IP receives the data, breaks it up into packets, and sends it to a network within the Internet.
Telnet	A program which allows users to remotely use computers across networks.
Text file	An unformatted file of text characters saved in ASCII format.
Thread	An ongoing message-based conversation on a single subject.
TIFF	Tag Image File Format - a popular graphic image file format.
Tool	Software program used to support Web site creation and management.
Toolbar	A bar containing icons giving quick access to commands.
Toggle	To turn an action on and off with the same switch.
TrueType fonts	Fonts that can be scaled to any size and print as they show on the screen.

UNIX Multitasking, multi-user computer operating system that is run by many computers that are connected to the Internet.

Upload/Download The process of transferring files between computers. Files are uploaded from your computer to another and downloaded from another computer to your own.

URL Uniform Resource Locator, the addressing system used on the Web, containing information about the method of access, the server to be accessed and the path of the file to be accessed.

Usenet Informal network of computers that allow the posting and reading of messages in newsgroups that focus on specific topics.

User ID The unique identifier, usually used in conjunction with a password, which identifies you on a computer.

Usenet The global news-reading network.

Veronica A search utility that helps find information on Gopher servers.

Virtual Reality Simulations of real or imaginary worlds, rendered on a flat two-dimensional screen but appearing three-dimensional.

Virus A malicious program, downloaded from a web site or disc, designed to wipe out information on your computer.

VRML	Virtual Reality Modelling Language. A way to describe "worlds" that are displayed in three dimensions for the user to "walk through" or "fly over."
W3C	The World Wide Web Consortium that is steering standards development for the Web.
WAIS	Wide Area Information Server, a Net-wide system for looking up specific information in Internet databases.
WAV	Waveform Audio (.wav) - a common audio file format for DOS/Windows computers.
Web	A network of hypertext-based multimedia information servers. Browsers are used to view any information on the Web.
Web Page	An HTML document that is accessible on the Web.
Webmaster	One whose job it is to manage a web site.
WINSOCK	Winsock - a Microsoft Windows file that provides the interface to TCP/IP services.
World Wide Web	See Web.
Zine	An electronic magazine accessed through the Web.
ZIP	A compressed file format (.zip). Many files available on the Internet are compressed or zipped in order to reduce storage space and transfer times.

APPENDIX A
HTML Code for Example Web Pages

Code for Page - index.htm

```
<HTML>
<HEAD>
<TITLE>Michael Strang - British oil painter of landscapes,
seascapes and flowers</TITLE>

<META NAME="Author" CONTENT="Phil Oliver">

<META NAME="Description" CONTENT="Site of Michael
Strang, the contemporary British artist who has exhibited
at both the Tate Gallery in St Ives and the Royal Academy in
London.">

<META NAME="KeyWords" CONTENT="artist, landscape,
seascape, Michael Strang, picture, oil painting, Cornwall,
Cornish art, painter, English, British, poppy, poppies">
</HEAD>

<!---Start Page Body--->
<BODY TEXT="#000000" BGCOLOR="#FFFFFF"
LINK="#0000EE" VLINK="#551A8B" ALINK="#FF0000"
BACKGROUND="background.gif">

<CENTER><!---Heading text with red colour--->
<H3><FONT COLOR="#FF0000"><FONT SIZE=+2>
MICHAEL STRANG
</FONT></FONT></H3>
</CENTER>

<CENTER><B>Michael Strang, the contemporary British
artist who lives in Cornwall, specialises in textured oil
paintings of seascapes, landscapes and flowers -
especially poppies.</B></CENTER>

<CENTER><!---Top left image code--->
<A HREF="beach.jpg"><IMG SRC="beachsm.jpg"
ALT="Porthcurno and Logan Rock, Cornwall" HSPACE=10
VSPACE=10 BORDER=0 HEIGHT=80
WIDTH=112></A> 
```

163

```
<!---Top right image code--->
<A HREF="poppy.jpg"><IMG SRC="poppysm.jpg"
ALT="Poppies on the edge of a Cornish cornfield"
HSPACE=10 VSPACE=10 BORDER=0 HEIGHT=80
WIDTH=112></A></CENTER>

<CENTER><!---Bottom left image code--->
<A HREF="moon.jpg"><IMG SRC="moonsm.jpg"
ALT="Gulval Sunflowers by Moonlight, Cornwall"
HSPACE=10 VSPACE=10 BORDER=0 HEIGHT=80
WIDTH=112></A> 

<!---Bottom right image code--->
<A HREF="rivusk.jpg"><IMG SRC="rivusksm.jpg" ALT="On
the River Usk, Near Tallybont, South Wales" HSPACE=10
VSPACE=10 BORDER=0 HEIGHT=80 WIDTH=112></A>
</CENTER>
<BR CLEAR=BOTH>

<!---Menu bar--->
<CENTER><FONT SIZE=+1>
<A HREF="artist.htm">About the Artist</A> |
<A HREF="gallery.htm">Gallery</A> |
<A HREF="http://www.michaelstrang.com">Main Site</A>
</FONT></CENTER><BR>

<!---Copyright message --->
<CENTER><FONT SIZE=-1>&copy; All pictures are the
copyright of Michael Strang the artist &copy;
</FONT></CENTER>

<!---Horizontal line--->
<HR WIDTH="50%">

<!---Page signature --->
<CENTER><ADDRESS><FONT SIZE=-1>
Site maintained by <A
HREF="mailto:prmolive@csm.ex.ac.uk">Phil
Oliver</A>.   Last modified on 28 July 1998
</FONT></ADDRESS></CENTER>

</BODY>
</HTML>
```

Code for Page - artist.htm

```
<HTML>
<HEAD>

<TITLE>Michael Strang - the British Artist - Career
Background</TITLE>

<META NAME="Author" CONTENT="Phil Oliver">

<META NAME="Description" CONTENT="Career details of
Michael Strang, the contemporary British artist and painter
of seascapes, landscapes, portraits and flowers.">

<META NAME="KeyWords" CONTENT="artist, landscape,
seascape, Michael Strang, picture, oil  painting, Cornish
art, painter, English, British, poppy, poppies, contemporary
art, gallery, galleries, flowers, sunflowers">

</HEAD>

<!---Start Page Body--->
<!---BODY tag also sets page element colours--->
<BODY TEXT="#000000" BGCOLOR="#FFFFFF"
LINK="#0000EE" VLINK="#551A8B" ALINK="#FF0000"
BACKGROUND="background.gif">

<!---Outer container table to limit width of page--->
<CENTER>
<TABLE BORDER=0 WIDTH=600 ALIGN="CENTER">
<TR>
<TD>

<!---Start of first image--->
<CENTER>
<A HREF="tate.jpg"><IMG SRC="tate.jpg" BORDER=0
HEIGHT=171 WIDTH=260 ALT="The artist with Tate Gallery
in background"></A><BR>
<FONT SIZE=-2><B>Michael Strang, St Ives - Tate Gallery in
background</B></FONT>
</CENTER>
<!---End of first image--->
```

```
<P ALIGN="JUSTIFY"><B>Michael Strang</B> has a
Diploma in Art and Design (Hons) London, and studied at
the Wimbledon and Camberwell Schools of Art.</P>

<P ALIGN="JUSTIFY">He lives in Cornwall and paints
landscapes, still lifes, portraits and other subjects, mainly
in oils, but sometimes water colour. <B>He accepts
commissions</B>, and his work can be found in various
collections in Canada, the USA, Switzerland, Germany,
Corsica and the United Kingdom.</P>

<!---Second image--->
<CENTER>
<IMG SRC="text.jpg" ALT="A painting is but a prayer"
HEIGHT=108 WIDTH=414>
</CENTER>

<P ALIGN="JUSTIFY">He has been painting since 1973,
supports many charitable causes and has shown in an
impressive list of galleries, including:</P>

<!---Start of nested table--->
  <CENTER>
  <TABLE BORDER=1  CELLPADDING=3
ALIGN="CENTER" >
  <TR>
    <TD>Royal Academy - London</TD>
    <TD>Tate Gallery - St Ives*</TD>
    <TD>Mall Gallery - London</TD>
  </TR>
  <TR>
    <TD>New Craftsman - St Ives </TD>
    <TD>CSM Gallery</TD>
    <TD>George Frederick Watts Gallery</TD>
  </TR>
  <TR>
    <TD>Member Chelsea Arts Club </TD>
    <TD>Cornwall Education Collection </TD>
    <TD>Bryan Forbes Gallery</TD>
  </TR>
  </TABLE>
  </CENTER>
<!---End of nested table--->
```

```
<P ALIGN="JUSTIFY">* A series of over 50 small
Porthmeor Paintings were shown at the Tate Gallery, St
Ives in their &quot;Century of Images&quot; exhibition
from April to October 1995.</P>

<!---Horizontal line--->
<HR size=3 width="250">

<!---Text menu bar --->
<CENTER><FONT SIZE=+1>
   <A HREF="index.htm">Home</A> |
   <A HREF="gallery.htm">Gallery</A> |
   <A HREF="http://www.michaelstrang.com">Main
Site</A>
</FONT></CENTER>

<!---Closing code for outer container table--->
</TD></TR>
</TABLE>
</CENTER>

<HR size=3 width="250">

<!---Page signature --->
<CENTER>
<ADDRESS><I>This page is maintained by <A
HREF="mailto:prmolive@csm.ex.ac.uk">Phil
Oliver<BR>
</A></I>Last updated 28 July 1998</ADDRESS>
</CENTER>

</BODY>
</HTML>
```

Code for page - gallery.htm

```html
<HTML>
<HEAD>

<TITLE>Michael Strang - the British Artist - Gallery</TITLE>

<META NAME="Author" CONTENT="Phil Oliver">

<META NAME="Description" CONTENT="Some work of the
contemporary British artist Michael Strang, who specialises
in seascapes, landscapes, portraits and flowers, mostly in
oils">

<META NAME="KeyWords" CONTENT="artist, landscape,
seascape, Michael Strang, picture, oil  painting, Cornish
art, painter, English, British, poppy, poppies, contemporary
art, gallery, galleries, flowers, sunflowers">
</HEAD>

<!---Start Page Body--->
<!---BODY tag also sets page element colours--->
<BODY TEXT="#000000" BGCOLOR="#FFFFFF"
LINK="#0000EE" VLINK="#551A8B" ALINK="#FF0000"
BACKGROUND="background.gif">

<!---Michael Strang, the contemporary British artist who
specialises in painting seascapes, landscapes, portraits
and flowers in oil --->

<!--- Adds a banner, linked to main site--->
<CENTER><A HREF="http://www.michaelstrang.com">
<IMG SRC="msbaner2.gif" ALT="Michael Strang - English
painter" HEIGHT=40 WIDTH=400 BORDER=0></A>
<BR><BR>

<!--- Red and large heading font--->
<B><FONT SIZE=+2><FONT COLOR="#ff0000">
GALLERY
</FONT></FONT></B><BR>

Click an image to open a larger view.<BR>
</CENTER>
```

```
<!---Code for menu bar --->
<CENTER><P><FONT SIZE=+1>
<A HREF="index.htm">Home</A> I
<A HREF="artist.htm">The Artist</A> I
<A HREF="http://www.michaelstrang.com">Main Site</A>
</FONT></P></CENTER><BR>

<!---Code to place first gallery image --->
<P></A><A HREF="beach.jpg"><IMG SRC="beachsm.jpg"
ALT="Porthcurno and Logan Rock" HSPACE=40
BORDER=0 HEIGHT=80 WIDTH=112 ALIGN=LEFT></A></P>

<!---Image text alongside image--->
<P><B>1   Porthcurno and Logan
Rock</B><BR>
Oil, 8 x 12 in.<BR>
Circa 1993;</P>
<BR CLEAR=BOTH><BR>

<!---Code to place second gallery image --->
<P></A><A HREF="poppy.jpg"><IMG SRC="poppysm.jpg"
ALT="Poppies on the edge of a Cornish cornfield"
HSPACE=40 BORDER=0 HEIGHT=80 WIDTH=112
ALIGN=LEFT></A></P>

<P><B>2  Poppies on the edge of a Cornish
cornfield</B><BR>
Oil, 24 x 36in.<BR>
1992-97; This painting has been worked on several times
over the last five years and has a superb 3-dimensional
texture.</P>
<BR CLEAR=BOTH>

<!---Code to place third gallery image --->
<P></A><A HREF="moon.jpg"><IMG SRC="moonsm.jpg"
ALT="Gulval Sunflowers by Moonlight" HSPACE=40
BORDER=0 HEIGHT=80 WIDTH=112 ALIGN=LEFT></A></P>

<P><B>3  Gulval Sunflowers by
Moonlight</B>
<BR>Oil, 36 x 48 in.<BR>
1997; Painted to assist their fundraising.</P>
<BR CLEAR=BOTH>
```

```html
<!---Code to place last gallery image --->
<P><A HREF="rivusk.jpg"><IMG SRC="rivusksm.jpg"
ALT="On the River Usk, Near Tallybont, South Wales"
HSPACE=40 BORDER=0 HEIGHT=80 WIDTH=112
ALIGN=LEFT></A></P>

<P><B>4  On the River Usk, Near Tallybont,
South Wales</B><BR>
Oil, 28 x 36 in.<BR>
1988;</P>
<BR CLEAR=BOTH>

<CENTER>
<P>Go to Michael Strang's <A
HREF="http://www.michaelstrang.com">main site</A> to
see more of his work.</P>
</CENTER>

<HR SIZE=3 WIDTH="250">

<!---Code for menu bar --->
<CENTER><FONT SIZE=+1>
<A HREF="index.htm">Home</A> |
<A HREF="artist.htm">The Artist</A> |
<A HREF="http://www.michaelstrang.com">Main Site</A>
</FONT></CENTER>

<HR SIZE=3 WIDTH="250">

<!---Page signature --->
<CENTER>
<ADDRESS><I>This page is maintained by <A
HREF="MAILTO:prmolive@csm.ex.ac.uk">Phil
Oliver</A></I><BR>
Last updated 28 July 1998</ADDRESS></CENTER>

</BODY>
</HTML>
```

APPENDIX B
HTML Special Characters

We include here a listing of special characters and the code that is required to place them in an HTML document.

!	&#33;	Exclamation mark
"	&#34;	Quotation mark
#	&#35;	Number sign
$	&#36;	Dollar sign
%	&#37;	Percent sign
&	&#38;	Ampersand
'	&#39;	Apostrophe (straight)
(	&#40;	Left parenthesis
)	&#41;	Right parenthesis
+	&#43;	Plus sign
,	&#44;	Comma
-	&#45;	Hyphen
.	&#46;	Period (fullstop)
/	&#47;	Solidus (slash)
:	&#58;	Colon
;	&#59;	Semi-colon
<	&#60;	Less than
=	&#61;	Equals sign
>	&#62;	Greater than
?	&#63;	Question mark
@	&#64;	Commercial at
[	&#91;	Left square bracket
\	&#92;	Reverse solidus (backslash)
]	&#93;	Right square bracket
^	&#94;	Caret
_	&#95;	Horizontal bar (underscore)
`	&#96;	Acute accent
{	&#123;	Left curly brace
|	|	Vertical bar
}	&#125;	Right curly brace
~	&#126;	Tilde
,	&#130;	Lower apostrophe
ƒ	&#131;	f symbol

„	&#132;	Lower inverted commas
...	&#133;	Dot dot dot
†	&#134;	single cross
‡	&#135;	Double cross
^	&#136;	Eastern European inflection
‰	&#137;	Extended percent sign
Š	&#138;	Eastern European capital S
‹	&#139;	Small less-than symbol
Œ	&#140;	Capital OE
‘	&#145;	Apostrophe (left)
’	&#146;	Apostrophe (right)
“	&#147;	Inverted commas (left)
”	&#148;	Inverted commas (right)
•	&#149;	Round bullet
–	&#150;	Hyphen
—	&#151;	Long hyphen
~	&#152;	Small tilde
™	&#153;	Trademark symbol
š	&#154;	Eastern European small S
›	&#155;	Small greater-than symbol
œ	&#156;	Lower case oe
Ÿ	&#159;	Y umlaut
		Non-breaking Space
¡	&#161;	Inverted exclamation
¢	&#162;	Cent sign
£	&#163;	Pound sterling
¤	&#164;	General currency sign
¥	&#165;	Yen sign
¦	&#166;	Broken vertical bar
§	&#167;	Section sign
¨	&#168;	Umlaut (dieresis)
©	&#169;	Copyright
ª	&#170;	Feminine ordinal
«	&#171;	Left angle quote, guillemotleft
¬	&#172;	Not sign
-	&#173;	Soft hyphen
®	&#174;	Registered trademark
¯	&#175;	Macron accent
°	&#176;	Degree sign
±	&#177;	Plus or minus
²	&#178;	Superscript two

³	&#179;	Superscript three
´	&#180;	Acute accent
µ	&#181;	Micro sign
¶	&#182;	Paragraph sign
·	&#183;	Middle dot
¸	&#184;	Cedilla
¹	&#185;	Superscript one
º	&#186;	Masculine ordinal
»	&#187;	Right angle quote, guillemotright
¼	&#188;	Fraction one-quarter
½	&#189;	Fraction one-half
¾	&#190;	Fraction three-quarters
¿	&#191;	Inverted question mark
À	&#192;	Capital A, grave accent
Á	&#193;	Capital A, acute accent
Â	&#194;	Capital A, circumflex accent
Ã	&#195;	Capital A, tilde
Ä	&#196;	Capital A, dieresis or umlaut mark
Å	&#197;	Capital A, ring
Æ	&#198;	Capital AE dipthong (ligature)
Ç	&#199;	Capital C, cedilla
È	&#200;	Capital E, grave accent
É	&#201;	Capital E, acute accent
Ê	&#202;	Capital E, circumflex accent
Ë	&#203;	Capital E, dieresis or umlaut mark
Ì	&#204;	Capital I, grave accent
Í	&#205;	Capital I, acute accent
Î	&#206;	Capital I, circumflex accent
Ï	&#207;	Capital I, dieresis or umlaut mark
Ð	&#208;	Capital Eth, Icelandic
Ñ	&#209;	Capital N, tilde
Ò	&#210;	Capital O, grave accent
Ó	&#211;	Capital O, acute accent
Ô	&#212;	Capital O, circumflex accent
Õ	&#213;	Capital O, tilde
Ö	&#214;	Capital O, dieresis or umlaut mark
×	&#215;	Multiply sign
Ø	&#216;	Capital O, slash
Ù	&#217;	Capital U, grave accent
Ú	&#218;	Capital U, acute accent
Û	&#219;	Capital U, circumflex accent

Ü	&#220;	Capital U, dieresis or umlaut mark
Ý	&#221;	Capital Y, acute accent
Þ	&#222;	Capital Thorn, Icelandic
ß	&#223;	Small sharp s, German (ss ligature)
à	&#224;	Small a, grave accent
á	&#225;	Small a, acute accent
â	&#226;	Small a, circumflex accent
ã	&#227;	Small a, tilde
ä	&#228;	Small a, dieresis or umlaut mark
å	&#229;	Small a, ring
æ	&#230;	Small ae dipthong (ligature)
ç	&#231;	Small c, cedilla
è	&#232;	Small e, grave accent
é	&#233;	Small e, acute accent
ê	&#234;	Small e, circumflex accent
ë	&#235;	Small e, dieresis or umlaut mark
ì	&#236;	Small i, grave accent
í	&#237;	Small i, acute accent
î	&#238;	Small i, circumflex accent
ï	&#239;	Small i, dieresis or umlaut mark
ð	&#240;	Small eth, Icelandic
ñ	&#241;	Small n, tilde
ò	&#242;	Small o, grave accent
ó	&#243;	Small o, acute accent
ô	&#244;	Small o, circumflex accent
õ	&#245;	Small o, tilde
ö	&#246;	Small o, dieresis or umlaut mark
÷	&#247;	Division sign
ø	&#248;	Small o, slash
ù	&#249;	Small u, grave accent
ú	&#250;	Small u, acute accent
û	&#251;	Small u, circumflex accent
ü	&#252;	Small u, dieresis or umlaut mark
ý	&#253;	Small y, acute accent
þ	&#254;	Small thorn, Icelandic
ÿ	&#255;	Small y, dieresis or umlaut mark

APPENDIX C
Internet File Formats

All of the file formats found on the Internet can be broken into one of two types: **ASCII** text files you can view with WordPad or Notepad, and **Binary** which contain non-ASCII characters and cannot be viewed.

We include here a guide to the most common Internet file formats with details of how some of them can be viewed, or played.

Plain Text (ASCII) Files:

.html/.htm   The language in which Web documents are authored. File type is ASCII and requires a Web browser like Explorer for viewing.

.txt   An ASCII text file which can be viewed with Notepad.

Formatted Documents:

.doc   Used for formatted ASCII text files, but also for documents created in Microsoft Word.

.pdf   Portable Document Format, a binary format developed by Adobe Systems, Inc. that allows formatted documents to be transferred across the Net so they look the same on any machine. Requires a Reader which is available directly from Adobe.

.ps   A PostScript file is unreadable except by a PostScript printer or with an onscreen viewer like Ghostscript.

Compressed and Encoded Files:

.arc   An old binary format for archiving and compression, which can be manipulated by several programs, including the original ARC, ARCE (also known as ARC-E), PKXARC, and PKUNPAK.

.arj   A binary format for MS-DOS machines, especially in Europe. You can use WinZIP, or Stuffit Expander for Windows.

.bin   A Macbinary II Encoded File requiring Stuffit Expander.

.exe   A DOS or Windows binary executable program or self-extracting file. Launched by double-clicking its icon.

.gz/gzip   The GNU Project's compression program, a binary format most commonly used for UNIX and PC files. Use WinZip which handles this format the same way as Zip files.

.hqx   A Macintosh binary file that has been converted into ASCII text so it can be safely transferred across the Net. Use BinHex13 (binhex13.zip) on a Windows PC to un-binhex it.

.sit   A Macintosh binary file that has been compressed using the Stuffit program. Use Stuffit Expander for Windows.

.sea   A Macintosh self-extracting binary archive file.

.tar/.tar.gz/.tar.Z/.tgz

These binary files are often found on Unix-based Internet sites. WinZip handles all these formats the same way as Zip files.

.uu

UUencoded binary file. Used to convert binary data into text so it can be sent via e-mail. Explorer automatically decodes this type. You can also use WinCode to UUdecode files in Windows.

.Z

A UNIX binary compression format. Use WinZIP to decompress and view files with this extension.

.zip

A common binary compression standard for DOS and Windows that uses the DOS utility PKZIP. These files can be decompressed on the PC with WinZIP.

Graphics Files:

.gif

The most common graphics file format (binary) on the Internet, it stands for Graphics Interchange Format. Explorer views these automatically, or you can use Lview Pro (lviewpxx.zip) on a Windows PC.

.jpg/jpeg/jfif

A popular binary compression standard used for photos and still images. Browsers view these automatically.

.tiff/.tif

A very large, high-resolution binary image format.

Sound Files:

.au/uLaw/MuLaw The most common sound format (binary) found on the Web.

.aiff/.aif A fairly common binary sound format found on the Web.

.ra Real Audio, a new binary audio format, which allows you to play sounds in real-time. Requires a Real Audio Player.

.wav The native sound format for Windows.

Video Files:

.avi The standard binary video format for Windows.

.mov/.movie A common binary format for QuickTime movies, the Macintosh native movie platform.

.mpg/mpeg A standard binary format for "movies" on the Internet, using the MPEG compression scheme. There are a variety of MPEG Players for Windows and an MPEG FTP Site that has a large collection of MPEG player resources for all platforms (Mac, Windows, and UNIX).

.qt Another extension that denotes a binary QuickTime movie file.

INDEX

NOTES

NOTES

NOTES

COMPANION DISC TO THIS BOOK

This book contains several example Web page listings. There is no reason why you should type them yourself into your computer, unless you wish to do so, or need the practice.

The COMPANION DISC comes with these listings, the site picture files as well as a shareware copy of HTML Notepad.

COMPANION DISCS for most books written by the same author(s) and published by BERNARD BABANI (publishing) LTD, are also available and are listed at the front of this book. Except for those marked with an *. **Make sure you fill in your name and address** and specify the book number and title in your order.

ORDERING INSTRUCTIONS

To obtain your copy of the companion disc, fill in the order form below, or a copy of it, enclose a cheque (payable to **P.R.M. Oliver**) or a postal order, and send it to the address given below.

Book No.	Book Name	Unit Price	Total Price
BP 433	Your own Web site...	£3.50	
BP		£3.50	
BP		£3.50	
Name .... Address		Sub-total	£.............
		P & P (@ 45p/disc)	£.............
		Total Due	£.............
Send to: P.R.M. Oliver, CSM, Pool, Redruth, Cornwall, TR15 3SE			

PLEASE NOTE

The author(s) are fully responsible for providing this Companion Disc service. The publishers of this book accept no responsibility for the supply, quality, or magnetic contents of the disc, or in respect of any damage, or injury that might be suffered or caused by its use.